Ralph R.

Joseph G. Dawson III, General Editor

EDITORIAL BOARD

Robert Doughty
Brian Linn
Craig Symonds
Robert Wooster

Tanks
on
the
Beaches

A Marine Tanker in the Pacific War

ROBERT M. NEIMAN

AND KENNETH W. ESTES

Texas A&M University Press   *College Station*

Library of Congress Cataloging-in-Publication Data

Neiman, Robert M., 1918–

    Tanks on the beaches : a Marine tanker in the Pacific war /

Robert M. Neiman and Kenneth W. Estes.—1st ed.

      p. cm.— (Texas A&M University military history series ; no. 85)

  ISBN 1-58544-240-2 (cloth : alk. paper)

    1. Neiman, Robert M., 1918– 2. World War, 1939–1945—Personal

narratives, American. 3. United States. Marine Corps—Officers—

Biography. 4. World War, 1939–1945—Tank warfare. 5. World War,

1939–1945—Campaigns—Pacific Area. I. Estes, Kenneth W.

II. Title. III. Texas A&M University military history series ; 85.

D811.N444A3 2002

940.54'5973'092—dc21   2002014510

All photographs are courtesy U.S. Marine Corps
unless otherwise indicated.

To Robert L. Reed

(1918–81)

Major, USMCR (Retired)

Platoon Leader

Executive Officer

Company Commander

and

to all the terrific marines

of C Company, 4th Tank Battalion

May, 1943–October, 1945

CONTENTS

ILLUSTRATIONS

LIST OF MAPS

PREFACE

This book happened because Robert M. Neiman published a short essay in the *Marine Corps Gazette* in December, 1998. In it, Neiman discussed the apparent historical cycle of tank training and the development of tactical doctrine in the U.S. Marine Corps. His chief concern was that the neglect of tank-infantry training he saw in the early days of World War II was being repeated in the contemporary Marine Corps. The essay caught my attention while, as a retired marine tank officer and historian, I was conducting research for a history of the Corps and its use of armored fighting vehicles. Neiman's descriptions of Great Pacific War island battles and his mention of some of the major figures in USMC tank development prompted me to contact him and probe his knowledge of the key people and issues related to this story.

The result has been a long and pleasant relationship between two veteran tank officers from different generations. The extent of Neiman's knowledge and experience far surpassed my greatest hopes. It soon became clear that he had seen not only considerable combat with USMC tank units, he also had witnessed most of the important developments of his service's fledgling tank arm. The obvious question surfaced one day in 1999 after a series of interviews in his home: Why had he not written his story? The answer was compelling. Neiman's friends and others who had heard him speak on ceremonial occasions and on battlefield tours that he and his wife, Suzy, had taken, had been urging him to write a book for more than a decade. However, he felt he lacked the training and experience as a writer needed to pull it off. Sensing that this rare "insider's story" had to be told—for its loss would leave a serious gap in our knowledge of the time and the key events and personalities with which Neiman had been involved—I offered to help. He then volunteered to undertake the task.

After finishing my work on the history of the Marine Corps's employment of armored fighting vehicles, I conducted a series of taped interviews with Neiman during 2000–2001.[1]

Bob Neiman was virtually "present at the creation" of the U.S. Marine Corps's tank arm, and in a few years became one of its best practi-
tioners, perhaps its most experienced combat commander. Serving in the
1st Marine Division at the beginning of the war, his tank unit did not go
to Guadalcanal, but Neiman went ashore there later, enduring Japanese
bombardments to gather information for his assignment as operations
officer of the new tank school being formed in California. There he
eventually formed and trained his own tank company, which he led
through four island battles with the 4th Marine Division, culminating in
the cauldron of Iwo Jima. After switching back to the 1st Marine
Division, he became one of the rare Marine Corps officers to serve in both
the Iwo and Okinawa campaigns, finishing the war as executive officer
and commanding officer of the 1st Tank Battalion as it moved from wartime missions to occupation and security duty in North China in 1946.

Neiman's Marine Corps tank service highlights the differences between the use of armored fighting vehicles in the Pacific and in Europe
during World War II. In 1939, the beginning moves of the war in Europe
brought an end to the tank experiments conducted during the preced-
ing decade. The German pattern of the all-arms formation consisting of
tanks; mechanized and motorized infantry, engineers, and artillery; and
motorized logistical support backed by tactical airpower, became the
new standard for the major warring powers. The development of tanks
and their components now settled upon three distinct classes of evolution: light, medium, and heavy tanks weighing approximately ten,
twenty, and fifty tons, respectively. Light tanks initially performed in
the cavalry role, whereas medium and heavy tanks were given the infantry support mission. Although armies expected the antitank gun to
dominate the battlefield as it had in the Spanish civil war, tank mobil-
ity, armor protection, and firepower had advanced sufficiently by 1940
such that a new paradigm operated. Instead of the machine guns and
light cannon of the previous decade, World War II tanks carried main
guns of up to 152-mm bore, numerous machine guns, and even flame
weapons or rocket launchers on occasion. Improved running gear and
specially designed or modified engines permitted speeds in excess of
twenty miles per hour. By the end of the war, armor protection had
exceeded the penetration power of all but the most unwieldy heavy
antitank artillery. Tank cannon had to penetrate their opposite
numbers' armor, and a number of specialized vehicles were created for
the direct fire support (assault guns, close support tanks), antitank (tank

hunters or tank destroyers), engineer, tank recovery, and antiaircraft roles. Most importantly, the operational doctrine for tank employment began to exploit not only the tank, but also accompanying mechanized troops of all arms, supporting aircraft, and a fluid command style that permitted the exploitation of breakthroughs or weaknesses in the opposition forces, such that systemic collapses could be inflicted upon whole field armies. By the war's end, the Russian, American, and British armored forces had all converted to and developed a level of mechanization at least equal to the German panzer formations. Tanks thus played key roles in both eastern and western European campaigns, as well as those in North Africa. However, they also found significant employment in southern Europe, India, and East Asia.

In contrast to the maneuvering of large-scale armored and mechanized formations that had occurred in Europe and North Africa, rarely were more than a few dozen tanks employed at the same time in the Great Pacific War. In Pacific amphibious operations, specialized ships and landing craft brought tanks ashore after ingenious amphibious vehicles stormed the beaches and overpowered initial inland positions. As the Japanese stiffened their island defenses in 1943 and later, the tank became an essential component of the landing force. Despite the intense air and naval bombardment of Pacific islands prior to amphibious assaults, the troops in the initial waves made little progress against surviving defensive weapons. The Marine Corps's decision to send tanks ashore early in the assault phase of the landing resulted in Japanese defenses being overcome more quickly and restored the offensive.

As much as the tank-aircraft team ushered in mechanized warfare in Europe in World War II, the tank-infantry team developed by the U.S. Marine Corps and U.S. Army spearheaded the Pacific island campaigns. In the Pacific, opposing tanks rarely fought each other, and when they did, the lightly built and armed Japanese tanks caused scarcely any damage. Japanese weaknesses in industrial production and raw materials kept them from fielding anything like the standard U.S. medium tank. The words of two of the opposing generals on Okinawa summarize this aspect of the Pacific War. Major General Lemuel C. Shepherd Jr., commander of the 6th Marine Division, said, "If any one supporting arm can be singled out as having contributed more than any others during the progress of the campaign, the tank would certainly be selected." The Japanese Thirty-second Army commander, Lt. Gen. Mitsuru Ushijima, concurred, saying, "The enemy's power lies in its tanks."

Neiman joined the new 4th Marine Division in 1943 and encountered these and other facets of the war as that division evolved from novice to highly experienced. At first, the Pacific island campaigns involved short and intense assaults, followed by months out of action before the next battle. The venue of the Central Pacific campaign then shifted from fighting isolated garrisons on the small islands of scattered coral atolls to exhausting and extensive struggles between multiple divisions of troops on each side, fought over larger islands containing greatly varied terrain. Finally, on Iwo Jima and Okinawa, he encountered the new Japanese defensive doctrines of prolonged attrition and resistance, calculated to wear down the Allies and save the home islands from invasion.

The number of English-language personal accounts of tank combat can be counted on one hand. Bob Crisp, a British army major, wrote an account covering his two months as a company commander in the Eighth Army in North Africa before being wounded.[2] The diary of Cpl. Keith Douglas gives his impressions as a tank commander through the fall of Tunisia, but he was killed at Normandy and never wrote a memoir.[3] Avi Kahalani describes his epic weeklong fight as a tank battalion commander on the Golan Heights in Israel's 1973 Yom Kippur War.[4] Ralph Zumbro's memoir is the rather stylized account of a U.S. Army tank commander in Vietnam.[5] Bertram A. Yaffe, a junior tank officer in the Marine Corps in World War II, wrote a narrative that featured some breathtaking incidents, yet left the reader strangely unfamiliar with tank operations.[6] Other so-called personal accounts of armored warfare have been written by commanders too high in rank to capture the sound and smell of tank combat. In an attempt to correct the lack of tank crew narrative from the Great Pacific War, Oscar E. Gilbert, a geologist and former marine artilleryman, recently collected the testimonies of veterans into a compendium in which he links the personal accounts of the fighting to his own narrative of the battles.[7]

General accounts of the ground fighting in the Great Pacific War range from the poignant reporting of journalists like Richard Tregaskis and Ernie Pyle to the curious mixed fiction and autobiography of William Manchester. Above all these works stands Eugene Sledge's memoir, a chronicle of unparalleled precision and honest description of battle at its most cruel.[8] It is the best record of the horror of the infantryman's fight in the Marine Corps campaigns in the Pacific.

Neiman's experiences with fighting machines spanned the gamut from the "toy tanks" of 1940, the turretless Marmon-Herrington tankettes, to the standard thirty-four-ton M4 Shermans employed later in the war. He and his men experimented with their vehicles, using field improvisations and also some new ideas from the ordnance depots, like the deadly flamethrower tanks he first employed on Iwo Jima. He also used the new equipment and made improvisations in the amphibious warfare doctrine that proved to be the centerpiece of U.S. strategy in the Great Pacific War. Neiman saw the war unfold from an ideal observer's position as a company commander or battalion executive officer.

Bob Neiman's life story, told in his voice, emphasizes his Marine Corps career of 1940–46, but also touches on the business success he experienced after the war. His narrative contains stirring and interesting accounts of the fighting in the Great Pacific War, as well as Marine Corps service throughout World War II, featuring the unique perspective of men fighting from armored machines in desperate battles against a determined enemy.

Kenneth W. Estes
Seattle, Washington

ACKNOWLEDGMENTS

We received considerable support from individuals and institutions during the years spent researching and preparing this work for publication. Barry Zerby (College Park, Maryland) and Trevor Plante (Washington, D.C.) of the Military Records Section of the National Archives and Records Administration rendered essential service. Danny A. Crawford, Robert V. Aquilina, and Lena M. Kaljot at the USMC Historical Center in Washington, D.C., also provided expert assistance.

Julian "Bud" Lesser, a retired Marine Corps major and documentary filmmaker, added some interviews of his own in support of the information collection effort. Donald Gagnon, friend, tanker, secretary, and magazine editor of the Marine Corps Tankers' Association gave generously of his time and advice, as did Oscar E. Gilbert, Charles B. "C. B." Ash, Louis Metzger, and Dan Shepetis. Allan R. Millett and Joseph H. Alexander read drafts and provided expert advice on this book, and the staff of Texas A & M University Press made the usual perils of publishing quite painless. Dale E. Wilson, who taught military history at West Point and served as an army tank officer, corrected our many infelicities of style and provided much assistance in preparing the manuscript for publication.

Robert M. Neiman   Kenneth W. Estes
Indian Wells, California   Seattle, Washington

TANKS
ON
THE
BEACHES

CHAPTER 1
The Early Days
1918–39

BOARD OF INVESTIGATION
convened within the
REAR ECHELON, FIRST MARINE DIVISION TROOPS
MARINE BARRACKS, QUANTICO, VIRGINIA
by order of
THE COMMANDING OFFICER (SENIOR OFFICER PRESENT)

To inquire into and report upon the damage to Marmon-Herrington
Tank, CTL-3A, Marine Corps Number T8.
June 24, 1941.

Examined by the recorder:
1.   Q. State your name, rank and present station.
     A. Robert M. Neiman, second lieutenant, First Scout Company,
Division Special Troops, First Marine Division, Fleet Marine Force,
Marine Barracks, Quantico, Virginia.
2.   Q. Describe the circumstances, as you know them, in regard to
the fire in tank T8 on June 23, 1941.
     A. Lieutenant Mattson and myself were proceeding along the road
running from Fuller Road to the Combat Area at approximately 10
miles an hour. . . .

nly twenty-two years of age, I had been an officer in the U.S. Marine Corps for just four months, and here I was testifying to a board and explaining the destruction of tank number eight in the Corps's slender inventory of forty-six of these machines of war.[1] One could say that this was not an auspicious beginning for a new officer. But I was really not at fault, and so the board ruled. I would like to think that I somehow made up for the loss of that tank in the following years.

One could easily say that I had no predestination to enter the Marine Corps. However, certain aspects of my early life certainly prepared me for military service, perhaps more than the average kid in America.

After I was born in 1918, my parents lived in Mount Vernon, New York, for two more years. They worked on Manhattan Island as professionals in the garment industry. My mother, Paula, later became a stylist for Maurice Rentner, one of the leading ready-to-wear manufacturers of ladies clothing. She handled a line of clothing with two or three dressmakers, and traveled to Paris annually for shows and to direct the designers into taking and modifying designs and trends that they would see. Right before the depression she had started her own design and manufacturing company, a partnership called Paula Neiman-Davidson. They were successful for a while, but went out of business in 1933. She joined Maurice Rentner at that time, and worked for them for about thirty years. My father, Irving Neiman, was also a manufacturer. He went into business in the 1920s with a company called Colony Club Frocks, which made more casual wear, and then formed I. C. Neiman, Incorporated. Both companies failed in the 1930s. He and his brother Ben then formed a partnership called Gramatan Dress Company on Gramatan Avenue in Mount Vernon. They supplied the Lerner Shops, a stylish clothing company for white-collar workers wanting professional clothing at lower prices. They made knock-offs of the better-selling department store dresses, manufacturing them at a reduced cost. They began to prosper in the latter part of the depression and did especially well during the war years.

My parents separated when I was fourteen and divorced when I was seventeen. Dad remarried almost immediately afterward, and upon my son John's birth in 1952 he and his wife moved to Van Nuys to be close to his grandson. He then bought into a partnership called California Foundations, which made foundation garments. Dad recognized that the petticoat generation was beginning and talked his partner into abandoning brassieres and going into petticoats and looser undergarments. They prospered with that for several years. He was around seventy years old by the time that boom busted, so he liquidated and retired. He kept busy in my lumber company, helping out with marketing until he passed away in 1968 at the age of eighty-three.

I went to summer camp for the first time at age six. It may have been a little early for me, but I did not know the difference. Camp Scataco was a very enjoyable and well-run camp, and I was the youngest of the "midget" campers. There were 250 campers in all. I loved being in a cabin with ten guys who were all able to play together. I learned to swim that first summer and had a great time. One time my parents came up, Mother later remembered, and they expected me to run over and throw myself in their arms. Instead, I filed past in my group on the way to some activity and only said, "Hi Mom!" She said it broke her heart to think that I apparently had not missed them. We played all sports, including boxing, and from then on I was always at summer camp. I spent only the first two years at Scataco. The thing I remember best is that the camp director and owner, Nat Holman, founded the New York Celtics as a player-coach, long before the advent of the National Basketball Association. All the counselors were college basketball players. Once each summer, the Celtics came to the camp to play. Nat always played center with the Celts, and I never could understand why our own director played against us!

Three years later, I went to Saint John's Military School in upstate New York for two academic years. I loved that, too, and I had a lot of interesting experiences. My roommate the first year, 1927, was Allan Crosland, whose father was a well-known movie director. I attended the junior school, one of the twenty or so kids of elementary school age. The bulk of the cadets were in the senior school. We would tag along when the big guys went into the bathroom, watch while they took a few puffs off a cigarette and then, when they were ready to throw it away and return to class, we would beg the butt off of them and have a few puffs ourselves. So we were smoking cigarettes at this age and really feeling big-time. When it came time to go home for Christmas break, Allan and I decided that we should procure our own cigarettes. Because there were no vending machines and stores would not sell to us, we decided to bring the other kids into our conspiracy. The plan was to loot our parents' cigarette boxes, typically on coffee tables in every home in those days. Although we talked all of the kids in the junior school into joining our project, only Allan and I actually did it. We returned to school loaded with stale cigarettes. We got all the kids into our room and we put a pile of cigs on a bed and started lighting up and throwing them out in the sink. By taps, everybody had left and we were lying there smoking up our cache. We sprinkled Rice Krispies in the hallway to alert us to anyone approaching in the corridor. All of the faculty members were reserve army officers with the exception of a few active-duty Reserve Officers Training Corps (ROTC) instructors. We heard the crunch, scrambled under our covers, and pretended to be asleep. I can still remember the voice of the instructor, anxiously calling out, "Where's the fire? Where's the fire?" We had been smoking so much that a cloud had wafted out under the door, attracting this unwanted attention. It did not take him very long to realize what had happened. He shook out Crosland, who was closest to the door, saying, "Who's been smoking?" I peeked out from under my covers and saw Crosland pointing at my bed. The officer let go of Allan, reached out, and pulled me out of the bed. The cigarettes hidden under my pillow spilled out as well. He dragged me in my pajamas down to the commandant's office. By then it was around 11 P.M. "There's no fire, sir, it was just this brat smoking," he told the commandant of cadets. This was a big thing, because even the seniors were not supposed to be smoking on campus. They called my parents, told them what had happened, and said they would have to come up and get me. However, my father must have convinced them to keep me and give me a second chance. I wound up serving two weeks' barracks arrest and never smoked again—until age sixteen, that is.

At graduation, the junior school cadets performed in a rifle drill contest. It was an elimination event. The officers judged us as we executed a variety of commands, tossing out anyone who made a mistake until the last junior cadet remained. It was me! Despite my disciplinary flaw, I won the contest and was immediately made a corporal on the last day of my first academic year. I went back the following year, a ten-year-old sporting two stripes on my sleeve. The following three years, however, I stayed at home, my parents having moved out of their fashionable apartment-hotel in Manhattan into an apartment big enough for me as well. So I lived and went to school in Manhattan at Public School 166. Then, as my parents approached the breakup of their marriage, I was sent to Riverside Military Academy in Gainesville, Georgia. It also had a winter campus in Hollywood, Florida. I always seemed to leave for

Me with Jean Elgart, my first girlfriend, at Saint John's Military School in 1929.
Author's collection.

school on my birthday, which fell on September 14, and I enjoyed both the Georgia and Florida campuses very much. The city of Hollywood had been laid out nine miles north of Miami as part of the 1920s real estate bubble, which by then had burst. The Hollywood Beach Hotel had been built on the east end of a broad avenue that ran three miles through a huge circle and park, crossed U.S. 1, and continued past stores, two railroad depots, and a very ornate city hall until it reached the west end of town, where there rose another magnificent hotel. This building had never opened, nor had the two-story school building nearby. Somehow the Chamber of Commerce convinced the Riverside Military Academy administrators that it would be a wonderful site, and they had acquired the vacant hotel and school that very year. So, after Christmas vacation, students reported to the winter campus, and in the spring we went back to Gainesville by train. That first year, 1932–33,

I did not go home for Christmas vacation but instead went on to the Florida campus with other kids who had similar arrangements with their parents. At our first train stop, we bribed the bellman for a bottle of moonshine. I nearly died after drinking from it, and I abstained for several years afterward. We had a ball in Miami, going to the dog races for New Year's Eve. Mother, now separated, and her sister Ruth, also recently divorced, came to Hollywood that year and stayed at the Hollywood Beach Hotel—no doubt both looking for a rich guy to marry. Indeed, my aunt caught one then and there.

When I look back on it, most of us kids felt great respect for our parents, but we all liked our time away from them. I saw Dad for a period in the summer of 1932, and then went to camp again. We had been using Camp Kokosing, in Vermont, but this time would be my last of seven consecutive summers spent there. My first year there was also the year the camp opened, so we had sort of grown up together. Although I was only fourteen, the counselors put me with the seniors because of my previous experience. While I was there I learned fencing from two counselors who played on the Columbia University fencing team.

Years later, in 1967, Suzy and I went with family to the Montreal Expo as the member of a business organization that had local members important in its running. On the way back, we stopped at Camp Kokosing and I was pleased to see the widow of the director still there running the place with one of her sons, who was my age. Kids were nicknamed at Camp Kokosing by switching the first letters of their names. I was "Nobby Beiman," which is just how she greeted me when she spotted me getting out of the car—after thirty-four years! We had a nice reunion and took a family swim before continuing on that same day. We also visited the Roxbury Prep School (now Cheshire Academy), where the headmaster, Arthur Sherrif, arranged for us to stay a couple of days. I tried hard, but I never could interest our boys in attending. However, we did meet Larry Kelly—an alumnus and an all-American at Yale and one of the first Heisman Trophy winners—and my son Phil loved throwing the football with him. That visit served to rekindle many of my memories of those places.

During my final summer at Kokosing, my fellow campers included guys up to eighteen years of age. It was the summer of 1933, in the worst depths of the Great Depression, and some Ivy League colleges, including Harvard, had students who openly joined the Communist Party. We had half a dozen Harvard freshmen at camp who were Com-

munists. Although they belonged to wealthy families, they had joined
a campus cell. I knew little about communism, but what I did know I
did not like. Our economic system was malfunctioning, and these guys,
whom I had known for seven years, wanted me to join their cell. I put
it off because I disliked their calling my father and mother "bosses" in
their jargon, even though they were not rich capitalists. Dad was a terrific guy and his workers loved him. I could not tolerate the dogma of
shooting the bosses when the proletariat took over. I just did not want
to be part of anything that was against my parents in any way, even as
independent of them as I was. Finally, at the end of summer, we (the
"seniors") went on a motor-hike trip, riding a truck to a mountain, hik-
ing it, and then going on to the next one. We hiked up Mount Mansfield,
Vermont's highest peak, from which, on a clear day, we could see the
Atlantic Ocean. I recall that at the top, "Tippy," the ringleader of the
communist cell, told me I had to sign up. He used the old phrase,
"comes the revolution, all bosses will be liquidated" and when he said
my Dad would have to go, too, I hauled off and hit him with all my
might. We never talked again, then or since. That turned out to be my
last summer as a camper, because my parents could not afford it
anymore. The next summer, 1934, I was a junior counselor at the
Mount Vernon YMCA Camp. My father had arranged it; I received no
pay, but it was a free summer camp. The next two summers, though, I
was a real counselor.

Thus, I never lived at home for very long, and was glad to go out on
my own. Nevertheless, my parents continued to influence my life and
character, each in their own way. My Dad was never particularly strict,
but he set an example as a kind, honorable person who made me understand that one went through life without lying, cheating, or stealing,
and so forth. My mother, on the other hand, was a stricter person. She
frequently criticized me, but in a positive manner, instilling in me a
feeling that I could be good at anything I wanted to do, while at the
same time, urging me to do more and better. This gave me a good measure of self-confidence. That confidence stayed with me through school,
the Marine Corps, and business.

In the years when I attended school at home, I heard all kinds of business discussions between my parents at dinner. They did not work in
the same line, but they would talk about the business, and I determined
then that whatever I did, it would not be in the dress business. Yet,
surely some notion of business as a career was imprinted on me back

then. I know that Dad would have liked me to join his company when I graduated from college. But I was very frank with him, saying that although I loved them both, I did not want to work or live with either one of them. Anyway, I did not like New York City and I did like the Washington, D.C., area.

My final years of schooling took place at Roxbury Prep in Cheshire, Connecticut. Later renamed the Cheshire Academy, it was founded in 1794 as the Episcopal Academy of Connecticut. It originally had the military orientation characteristic of most private boarding schools. Right after World War I a group of faculty members at Yale saw a need for a school to tutor students for Yale. They believed in small classes and I never saw more than eight of us together. I found myself with only one other guy in a course in modern European history. The other guy was ill for most of the semester, so I attended the class by visiting the old professor in his quarters, where we sat in armchairs in front of a fireplace.

They gave us a lot of homework at Roxbury because the main objective was to teach us how to study. With such heavy homework assignments and so few students in a class, any lack of preparation became obvious to the professors, who remanded slackers to the study hall, leaving them no time free in the evening. That meant no free time to go into town for a burger and a milk shake or coffee, listening to the radio in one's room, and so forth. That made for a considerable loss, so most of us tried to avoid study hall and did learn to study.

Roxbury was no longer a military school, although as an Episcopal school it remained very strict. Still, I had no trouble with the mandatory ROTC program when I began my studies at the University of Maryland. We had very little military science instruction in the military prep schools, but the key points of military routine, team play, and drill that I had accumulated in years of prep schools and summer camps placed me in a fine position. Although I signed up as a business major, the curriculum remained the same for all of us the first two years.

The main reason I went to the University of Maryland was fencing. I played and made captain on the fencing team at Roxbury, which then was closely aligned with Yale in sports. Back then, the Ivy League had big teams in every sport and operated a huge recruiting effort. However, they required students to have fifteen college-board credits to gain admission, so there was always a group of potential athletes who needed to go to places like Roxbury to prepare for the college boards. Because of the large number of athletes enrolled there, we had varsity, junior varsity, and third teams, and the varsity team was composed almost entirely of kids already signed to college scholarships. All the coaches also held positions at Yale.

Accordingly, Roxbury's varsity team played only college freshmen teams, not other high schools or prep schools. Since all colleges had a three-year limit in those days, the Roxbury experience proved very useful for them. We played against West Point, Annapolis, and the Ivy League schools' freshmen during the regular season. The varsity football team won most of its games, but I played on the junior varsity squad against other Northeast prep schools. Among the coaches was Yale's fencing coach, Robert Grasson of Belgium, who was also the U.S. Olympic team foil coach.

Fencing became a sport from the desire of noblemen in the Middle Ages to become proficient with the rapier. In order to do that, they had to devise a method of teaching with a training weapon, the foil. This weapon has a long, flexible "blade" with a button at the end. The rules emphasize good right of way and fouls, with a relatively small target on the body for scoring. Thus we have the sport of foil fencing. The object is to stick the other guy and not be stuck yourself. At the same time, the military weapon of the cavalry evolved as the saber, with both a point and a cutting edge. A little freer in its use, the saber has an increased target area and more ways to cut and thrust. In later years, the épée or dueling sword was developed and the sport again expanded to accommodate it. Thus the three weapons of the sport of fencing: foil, saber, and épée.

When I was fifteen and in my first year at Roxbury, I fenced in the all-Northeast prep championship. One match, fencing against a big guy, I made a mistake when lunging and bent over instead of remaining upright. The guy jumped up, hit me right on the back of the head, just below the mask, and knocked me down and unconscious. I learned never to do that again! My Dad had been a fine amateur boxer and took me to a number of bouts. He had boxed Golden Gloves and in a number of amateur levels in New York and apparently was quite good as he had a number of trophies. Anyway, it carried over and boxing was one of my favorite sports. I tried boxing at the University of Maryland, training at 140 pounds. Although I worked out with the team a number of times, I had to do fencing on the scholarship and I could not handle both at the same time.

During my senior year at Roxbury, Grasson read a letter to the fencing squad from the University of Maryland athletic director saying that he wanted a student-coach who would teach fencing to physical education majors. They offered a scholarship to come and teach part-time. My roommate, Cable Starlings, was interested in going, but he already had a football scholarship to some Ivy League school. He said to me, "Why don't we tell Grasson we will both do this; I'd like to go to Maryland and play football there." We were invited down to Maryland for a weekend and went with a number of others there as prospects. Cable played many sports well, including football, track, and saber fencing. He was a year older than me and had a six-foot-three-inch, 230-pound frame, making him a hot prospect for most colleges. Maryland gave me one of the greatest weekends of my life. It was the spring of 1935 and I was still only sixteen years old. The varsity football players were each assigned to take two of us that weekend and show off the place. The varsity quarterback, a guy named Sachs, drew us, and we slept in the team dorm, met all the guys, and went to the Saturday night dance with dates arranged with some Maryland coeds. We saw a Maryland–Johns Hopkins lacrosse match, a baseball game, a track meet, and we had tickets to all these events. I signed up and Starlings received a football scholarship there as well. They even threw in free laundry! At Maryland we not only did the classes in the Physical Education (PE) Department, we also decided, on our own initiative, to build a fencing team and to teach a new class in foil for the girls. We built a men's fencing team that first year, with no schedule for competition, just holding practice after class. We got about twenty-five to thirty guys on the squad, and we sold all the men their equipment, serving as intermediaries for Bob Grasson on commission. The university also bought equipment for the PE classes and for an eventual extramural sport.

We now expanded and started a girls club, getting about fifty coeds signed up. We began holding classes for them two nights per week. "Smoke" Mackert, the athletic director, arranged for our men's team to fence against two local colleges, probably to see if we really knew what were doing. We won both of the meets, much to his satisfaction. The only problem at that point was my roommate. He had fallen in love with a freshman girl, spent every night with her, refused to study, and flunked out. So I worked alone my sophomore year, and built a club team from the veterans of the previous year's team and some new guys. Meanwhile, Dr. Mackert scheduled meets with about eight local colleges. In the end, we won five and lost three, and received an invitation to the Mid-Atlantic Collegiate Fencing Championship at Johns Hopkins University in the spring. I got permission to take the team and recalled it during the postseason for more practice. We won the tourney and I won the individual saber championship as a playing coach. They gave us a big trophy of a musketeer, called the "Little Iron Man," and I brought it into the athletic director's office. He was delighted. At that point, Dr. Mackert designated us a varsity sport and we had a full schedule to play each year starting in 1937.

The team did very well in my junior year, winning all but one meet, which we lost by a single point to William and Mary College. The team that I formed in my senior year had some special talent: Andre Deladier, the son of the Naval Academy fencing master and a freshman at Maryland! We rushed him into my fraternity as well, and he proved to be a big boost for the team. He also helped with coaching and we arranged to practice one day a week against the Naval Academy squad, which we did not play normally. That really advanced our proficiency. The year after I graduated, Deladier continued to coach the Maryland team and take it three times per week to the Naval Academy, where his dad coached our players privately and continued the workouts with the Annapolis teams. My efforts to organize the team, teach fencing, and coaching all helped me very much, I am convinced, in later life—be it in the Marine Corps or civilian business. It also gave me great experience in leading people, often with surprising results. My sophomore year, a guy came out for fencing and caught on very quickly with the saber, but missed a whole week of practice. One day, I spotted him across campus. I ran over and read him the riot act, saying, "What the hell have you been doing?" and so forth. He looked at me and said, "I've never seen you in my life!" It turned out the guy was the twin brother of my fencer. This second twin brother then came out for the team (the first one never returned), and he went on to be my second in saber for the championship team.

The women also did very well. The year after I graduated, I continued coaching women's fencing for a small salary, and I also coached at a small women's college or finishing school in Washington (for $200; not a bad salary in those days). The University of Maryland team became a contender in the Southern Conference, with North Carolina as a prime opponent. We at Maryland became the unofficial champ, unofficial because we had no final tournament. We beat everybody except

William and Mary, with which we split (we played twice per year). The following year, there was a tournament and Maryland won. We also won the women's tourney. In the spring of 1940, I went to the University of North Carolina's Pan-Hellenic weekend, which also hosted the women's Southern Conference fencing tourney. Bandleader Kay Kaiser, a famous UNC alumnus was supposed to play for the dances. It was a festive weekend, with parties everywhere. But Kay Kaiser took sick and somebody had to substitute for him. The unknown guy took the place by storm. His name was Glenn Miller, and he was just starting out. That was where he began his climb to fame.

The University of Maryland, being a land-grant college, featured mandatory ROTC for all male students during the first two years. This training proved to be very basic for me after my years of military prep schools. I quickly demonstrated that I knew at least as much about their simple drills as did the seniors. Little did I know that this time, my confidence would be my undoing. I had not yet declared a major, and was interested in both business and journalism. The English composition class, one of my favorites, met on Monday, Wednesday, and Friday afternoons. Friday was theme day. My military science class also met on Friday, but in the late morning, so I used to skip military science and lunch each Friday to work on my theme. I never skipped if there was a test, however, and I always scored an A. Near the end of the term, the professor of military science, an army colonel, called me into his office. After I reported, he said to me, "We are puzzled, you get As but have a lot of absences." He then told me that army regulations required that he take three points off my final grade for each class missed, leaving me with an F for the term. I could not believe it; I would have to repeat military science! I thus became the only sophomore in freshman ROTC, and the only junior in sophomore ROTC. I otherwise kept above-average grades at Maryland, but I really did not like it later when I had to tell the headmaster at Roxbury why I failed ROTC. At that time, the top ROTC grads at the University of Maryland typically went into the Marine Corps. These included guys like Lou Ennis, the big, good-looking president of the senior class and student body, an all-American lacrosse player and all-South football player who had even become engaged to the homecoming queen to finish the big-man-on-campus stereotype. Ennis ruled as the campus hero my first year and then went into the Corps, as did one of my best friends, Tom Fields, with whom I have remained close ever since.

Graduation in 1939 brought me to several points of decision at the
same time. The United States began training a team for the 1940 Olym-
pics, to be held at Helsinki, Finland. I spent June working out daily in
New York City with the saber, and the coach offered me a place on the
U.S. Olympic team. The business career for which I had prepared myself took precedence, however. On July 5 I traveled back to Washington,
D.C., to report to work with the Equitable Life Assurance Society. Fencing continued to hold my interest, though, and I later worked out with
a Hungarian master in New Zealand in 1942 and continued after the
war with the Los Angeles Athletic Club. My competitive fencing came
to a close about 1950. I liked fencing so much because it was a mental
game as well as physical, and I suppose that it must have been an in-
tuitive preparation for combat. But that possibility remained beyond
even my imagination at the time.

The recruiters who came to the University of Maryland business
school offered various opportunities to those of us who had majored in
marketing and finance and I seemed to receive a lot of interest from
them. Most offered good jobs with big companies, but I was attracted
to the Equitable because it had a program that would allow me to begin accumulating the capital I knew I would need for my own business.
The Equitable people also gave psychological tests to interviewees to
determine how well we were suited to selling and marketing. Believe
it or not, they said that I was the best of the test group and they offered
me a job, which entailed my returning to New York City for training
for a year. The Equitable people told me that they looked for people who
"partly" had worked through school and managed to participate in ex-
tracurricular activities as well, resulting in a more well-rounded person
than somebody who had simply stayed in school. Going back to New
York City did not attract me at all, and I managed to convince them
that I could train in the Washington office and perform my job right
there, in the city where I already enjoyed so many friends and good
times. I would be able to spend the next year concentrating on my business career and social life, with no other interferences—or at least so it
seemed to me then.

CHAPTER 2

Joining Up, but with Whom?

majored in business management at the University of Maryland's College of Commerce and Public Administration. I had no intention of returning to New York City, which I did not like and where I had only lived for about three years anyway. Dad wanted me to join his business as a salesman, but I wanted nothing of the rag business. The Equitable's new program called for developing a professional life insurance sales staff. Historically, a person went into life insurance sales because he had failed at something else. He then sold policies to all of his extended family and friends. That was about all he could do. But it had become a very technical business, and the Equitable wanted to build a professional sales force. They had the very first such program, and I joined it in its first year. They also had a management program, but I wanted to become independent, so I chose the six-month sales course with the intent of making enough capital to launch myself on my own later.

With my parents suffering financially because of the depression, I knew that I would have to build my own capital for any personal venture. The salaries offered by this firm would support my initial living setup in Washington, D.C., and the commissions I would likely make would then go toward creating the capital I would eventually need. The Equitable established its professional sales training program in an attempt to standardize and improve its performance in a relatively unorganized business area. The course took one year and I would continue to work under the "wing" of a manager for fieldwork. By the end of the year, I would be working solely for commissions.

Rather than go after the rich and already successful clients, I formed a different strategy and niche in the sales end of the business. This consisted of spotting talented young college grads who perhaps would make it big and make them clients. If they prospered, then I would as well. I joined the Washington, D.C., Junior Chamber of Commerce (Jaycees) as part of this strategy, and by 1940 I was doing great, earning about $50 per week—perhaps more than most of my classmates at Maryland. While this seemed to be a great basis for business, I saw some other complications. In 1940, the European war seemed to worsen and the United States began to rearm and prepare. The National Guard was called up for a year and there was talk of an imminent draft, which Congress debated vigorously. As long as the national service obligation for men aged twenty-one to thirty-five would be only one year, it seemed to me that I ought to get my service behind me as soon as possible, leaving the way clear for my career. I discussed it with my boss, David Bethune, who agreed with my judgment at the time.

We never had any trouble finding top speakers for our Jaycees meetings, and many of them came from the Congress or administration. We thus felt very close to the issues and before Congress voted on the draft, we took a straw vote. The vote was overwhelmingly in favor of America's first peacetime draft, even though our ages made us highly eligible for it. I went to the army and navy recruiters. The army wanted three-year volunteers and the navy wanted theirs to serve four. A friend of mine told me about the navy's V-12 program for college graduates. I spent an hour with the navy recruiter talking about it before I found out that I would be obligated to three years of service as a reserve officer. My boss, Dave, offered to help me find a program where I could take care of my obligated service but only spend about a year doing it. Within a day, he had discovered a Marine Corps program aimed at commissioning six hundred new second lieutenants fast to help the Corps meet the requirements for an expanded force. The Marine Corps planned to convene three Officer Candidate Classes (OCC) of four hundred men each, with a 50 percent planned dropout rate, to meet this need. The program called for seven months of training followed by six months of active duty in a combat unit. At that point, officers commissioned through the program would return to reserve status and be called up only in time of war or "national emergency." The first of these classes convened on November 1, 1940. I was attracted to the marines because they were an elite unit, and this program seemed just the right amount of time for my needs. I filled out the application forms.

In the middle of September I received word that I had been selected to participate in the first OCC, subject to passing a navy physical. I was in great shape, except that I used glasses for reading. My boss told me they would insist on 20/20 uncorrected eyesight, so he called a friend of his who was an ophthalmologist and asked him to see me that same day. I told the doctor that I had to pass the examination without exception or waiver. He pronounced me as being close in one eye, but not in the other. My problem, he said, was the strength of my focal powers, and he gave me a series of exercises to perform twice a day for the next six weeks. I did these twice a day and modified my diet as he directed. By the third day, he had me reading the 20/20 line on his eye chart. We continued this regimen until it was time for the physical, and then three more weeks thereafter for good measure. I passed the exam without a hitch, and when the time came to pay him for his services, he demurred, telling me that "anyone crazy enough to do all this to get into the U.S. Marines" would receive no bill from him. I never had a problem with vision throughout my active service, and it was not until nine years later, after I had begun having headaches, that I resumed using reading glasses.

In addition to my eye problems, I was engaged when I joined the marines. The Washington-Baltimore area contained several finishing schools for women of wealthy families to learn social graces and earn a degree. One of these was the Marjorie Webster School. When I was a junior at Maryland, one of my fraternity brothers brought this absolute knockout of a girl to a dance. I danced with her a lot that night and immediately fell for her. I asked her date later how much she meant to him and he said he did not know because it was their first date. However, he told me that it was all right with him if I asked her out. We quickly became an "item." When she did not return for my senior year, I hit it off with her roommate, Mary Mendenhall. Mary and I decided to marry later, and that she would stay in D.C. She found work in a May Company department store's College Shop. They wanted an all-American looker who could run the department. I got her the interview, and she landed the job.

We went to Wrightsville Beach, North Carolina, for two weeks in the summer of 1940 so I could meet her family. I was twenty-one and it was a wonderful summer. That was when I decided to get my selective service out of the way, as I described earlier. I called Mary and thought she would greet the news by exclaiming "My hero!" or some such thing, but her reaction was just the opposite. She was absolutely pissed off. "You can't do that," she snapped. "It's either me or the Marine Corps." She may have thought that I was bluffing and decided to call me on it. We broke up. I thought about her a lot. She was so pretty, bright, and talented. In the fall of 1941, while I was stationed at the Marine Corps base at nearby New River, I called Mary's former roommate in Wilmington, North Carolina, and talked to her mother. She told me that her daughter had gotten married and stayed in Wilmington, but said she was sure she would like to see me. They invited me to come down the first weekend I had available. We had a nice reunion and she arranged a date for me. She vowed that she would fix things with Mary. She said she would put on a house party, invite Mary, and get us back together by telling her she had a blind date for her. I really looked forward to our reunion, but during my next visit she told me that Mary had demanded to know who the blind date was and, upon learning the truth, said flatly, "I'm not coming."

I was sworn into the Marine Corps on November 14, 1940. The 1st OCC, which formed that month at Quantico, Virginia, showed me a lot about the military that I might only have imagined. I later learned that the Corps assigned some of its finest officers and NCOs to work with us. The commanding officer of Marine Corps Schools was Col. Lemuel C. Shepherd, and Maj. Gerald Thomas served as his executive officer and commanded the first candidate class. These two became, in a very short number of years, living icons of the postwar Marine Corps. We mostly trained with our sergeants, however, and they proved strict and demanding, but fair. Of the officers, we mostly saw Gerry Thomas. Thomas, for instance, commanded us in our march at President Roosevelt's inaugural parade on March 20, 1941. We had several other famous instructors, including Majs. Merrill Twining, Walter W. Wensinger, and Robert E. Hogaboom, who later became, like Thomas, senior generals in the postwar Marine Corps. Shepherd later served as commandant of the Marine Corps from 1952–55. Our noncommissioned officer (NCO) instructors tended to be mostly experienced gunnery sergeants, senior men who had fought in the banana wars and seen

**The 1st Officer Candidate Class, Maj. Gerald Thomas, commanding, is
shown in the battalion mass formation used when the unit marched in
Pres. Franklin D. Roosevelt's inauguration parade, March 20, 1941.**

duty with the fleet. Thomas told us they had combed the Corps world-
wide for instructors to make sure this experimental program worked.
For instance, one such man, a gunny named Feeney, was a perennial
champion of the national rifle match at Camp Perry. He served as our
chief rifle instructor. Having spent so much time in military school,
firing a rifle from the proper position was easy for me and Feeney kept
using me as a demonstrator model on the teaching platform. The story
went that Feeney had meticulously cleaned everything in his rifle before the final round one year at Camp Perry. However, he misjudged the
time and had to fire before he could zero the weapon. He still won.

The day before our graduation and commissioning as second lieutenants, Thomas called us together. I will never forget his words: "Gentlemen, the president through the secretary of the navy has informed the
Major General Commandant of a national emergency." He explained to
us that all reservists would remain on active duty for the duration. Thomas told us that the law invalidated the original offer made to us officer
candidates requiring only thirteen months' service. Nevertheless, he
said, the Marine Corps believed that it should keep its word to us. He
paused and looked around the room, then said that he would accept any
requests to drop the course. Any of us who wanted to could leave the
next day. The room fell silent. We had been so brainwashed by the train-

ing and wanted our commissions so badly that no one took him up on the offer.

So we finished out the course and went on to attend the 4th Reserve Officers' Class (ROC) as brand-new second lieutenants. Although the commander of this course was Lt. Col. Evans Ames, we all fell under the charge—one might say the spell—of yet another Marine Corps icon: Maj. Merrill Twining. Twining was one of the most brilliant officers to ever serve in the Corps. I can still remember a hike we took with him to the Manassas battlefield. We hiked the twenty miles to Manassas in full packs, listened to the briefings, walked the ground, and learned the use of terrain in military tactics and maneuver. At chow time, it began to rain. Twining remained outside, sitting on a fence and chewing on a piece of grass, while we lined up and went through the service line in the shed set up for the meal. After the last of us received our meal, the major came over to the shed for his chow. Nothing was said, but his actions illustrated better than all the lectures we attended how a marine officer looks out for his troops before himself. Twining stressed to us: "Take care of your people and they will take care of you. The troops get fed first, then the officers."

The other memorable part of our training with the 4th ROC was our orientation trip to the 1st Scout Company tank park. The 1st Marine Brigade left Quantico and trained in Cuba in 1940. It returned on paper

**Machine-gun training for newly commissioned
reserve officers at Quantico, Virginia.**
Author's collection.

**Marine Corps Reserve officers pass in review during their gradua-
tion ceremony at Quantico, Virginia.**

as a division in April, 1941. Now, after being ordered to Parris Island
to fill out its ranks, only the Division Special Troops remained at
Quantico. The sight of the tanks scooting around the field thrilled me,
and I crawled all over them, inside and out. The idea of remaining at
Quantico, so close to Washington and its social possibilities, also attracted me. Both John "Tex" Gillespie and I put in for duty with tanks
since we had decided to hang together after the course, and we received
orders instructing us to report to the 1st Scout Company, 1st Marine
Division, in June.

CHAPTER 3

First Organizations

Preparing for War

y real life as a Marine Corps officer began in June, 1941, when I was assigned to my first real unit with officers and men, a mission, and equipment. There I found the challenges that give a new officer a chance to prove himself and gain invaluable experiences in the process. It was my good fortune to serve under Capt. Henry W. Buse, a Naval Academy graduate and a superb and conscientious leader of marines. Bill Buse, who had been in command of the 1st Scout Company since November, 1940, became my true military mentor, and we stayed in touch long after I left active duty. He eventually rose to the penultimate heights in the Marine Corps command structure, serving as the three-star general commanding the Fleet Marine Force, Pacific, during the last years of the Vietnam War.

Originally formed in 1937 as the Corps's first tank company, the outfit had been redesignated in November. The scout company was uniquely designed for a form of mobile warfare like the army was planning, especially after observing the actions of the German army in the opening blitzkrieg campaigns of the war in Europe. The company had three platoons of four-wheel drive M3A1 scout cars, a platoon of light tanks, and a motorcycle platoon. Buse assigned me to command the motorcycle platoon and introduced me to my platoon sergeant,

"Muscles" Treadwell. Between the two of them, I became a true-blue Marine Corps officer, as Buse raised me from a pup and my platoon sergeant, Arthur "Muscles" Treadwell, showed me the basics in his own tough, gritty fashion.

I had never ridden a motorcycle before, but they needed an officer—even though Muscles was running the platoon just fine by himself. Treadwell taught me how to ride, but best of all, he taught me how to run a platoon of marines. He was a career marine from Maine—tall, wiry, thirty-five years old, and very salty. He did not take anything from any of the men, but they respected his know-how. He could be very sarcastic, and did not like lieutenants, but he apparently saw something in me. Under his direction, the platoon was always snappy in appearance and he ran it strictly. I had him for almost four months before he became the company first sergeant.

After this brief period of "growing up," I was ready for a tougher assignment, such as being the officer in charge of the slow troop train to New River, North Carolina, when the Division Special Troops moved there from Quantico to unite with the rest of the 1st Marine Division. The other officers traveled separately, in their cars, and Muscles drove mine down while I suffered through a very long day on a horrible old train. We sat in wooden cars moving at only twenty-five to thirty miles per hour from Quantico to Wilmington. There we changed to a badly maintained spur leading north to the New River estuary and the new Marine Corps camp there, the present-day Camp Lejeune. This "base" turned out to be nothing but some tent cities set in fields that had been freshly carved out of the woods. The enlisted men lived in pyramidal troop tents and the officers lived in two-man tents. Some concrete blockhouses contained the showers and we had canvas mess tents to complete the facilities that lined each "city" block. It was in this primitive setting that we undertook the huge task of creating a combat organization larger than any the Marine Corps had ever fielded.

Buse showed me right away that he was a wonderful guy with a terrific sense of humor. He taught me not to take myself too seriously and to employ humor frequently to relieve the pressure that builds up when troops are in a tight situation. Although he was teaching me how to be a good platoon leader, I was really learning from him how to be a company commander—and he sure knew what he was doing. Treadwell also taught me how to get results from the troops, but in a markedly different way: getting familiar with them while still keeping separate as an

**Here I am in 1941. I was running an errand in Quantico,
Virginia, and gave some neighborhood kids a ride
on my military WLA Harley-Davidson.**
Author's collection.

officer. Buse really fostered a brotherhood in the scout company, and in doing so he could also take advantage of our status as a separate unit.

I was fortunate to have him as my first commander, after whom I could model myself, but I also received my share of corrections. For instance, when the officers from the 5th ROC arrived at New River in advance of the additional troops for the new division being formed, they were initially assigned to the existing units as assistant platoon commanders because the regiments had not yet received their men and the separate battalions, like the 1st Tank Battalion, had not filled their additional companies. Second Lieutenant Webb Sawyer became my assistant platoon leader and three others took similar posts in the company: 2d Lts. Lew Griffin, Jack Hudson, and Tom O'Mahoney. All of them survived the war, and all had great careers in the Marine Corps. I remember walking with Buse from the post exchange (PX) back to bivouac, and I wanted to say something about the new guys. I started to say, "The *junior* officers did this," and he stopped and stared at me. "What did you say?" he asked. I started again and he said, "That's enough, who are you referring to?" I told him, and he said, "Who do you think *you* are? *You* are a junior officer!" That was a quick lesson in humility.

We all visited the Buses at home. They lived in the tall brick apartments up on the hill near the officers' club at Quantico, not the single-family homes with wood siding. I was there three or four times for dinner. He would frequently ask one of us to come to a meal and bring one or more of the other platoon leaders, or the executive officer, 1st Lt. Reed Fawell. I have no idea how Buse came to the scout company, but he and Charles G. "Griff" Meints—a school-trained tank officer who commanded it earlier and who later formed the 3d Tank Company and finally the 1st Tank Battalion—were close, so maybe he led him to it.

■ ■ ■

Captain Buse pulled me aside one day and said, "You are going to learn to drive a tank today." He had previously told me that he expected all of his officers to know how to drive every vehicle in the company. We had only five of these little tanks in the scout company. They were really baby tanks, and each was named after one of the Dionne quintuplets.[1] Second Lieutenant Robert B. "Bruce" Mattson, the tank platoon commander, drove up to the company office in a tank named "Marie" and told me to hop inside. I recall that we filled up with about eighty gallons of one-hundred-octane aviation gas drawn from the base air station, and then headed down the main base road to the combat range.

The Marmon-Herrington CTL-3 was very small, a five-ton vehicle with about the same amount of armor as a scout car—no more than half an inch of armor plating. A turretless two-man tank, it had a Lincoln V-12 engine that drove a rubber band track over a quadruple bogie-wheel suspension and moved at the very respectable speed of thirty-three miles per hour. It was equipped with dual driving controls—accelerator, gearshift, and steering brake levers—and had no periscopes, just vision

**A Marmon-Herrington CTL-3A light tank similar to my ill-fated "Marie"
is shown here in a publicity shot with one of the early LVT-I amphibian
tractors. The early threat of war saved us marines from
outfitting ourselves with a full complement of these baby
tanks. What a disaster that would have been!**

slits cut in an armored flap that could be opened for greater visibility. The only access was via a hatch on top. Even though it used a truck differential, it could spin like a top and maneuver very well. This made it a good reconnaissance machine, as it helped to be able to reverse and pull out of a hot situation. Inside the fighting compartment, the two crewmen each had a .30-caliber machine gun in a swiveling ball mount in front of him. In between them was a .50-caliber heavy machine gun. It was so long that the receiver extended past us. One of us was supposed to fire it by reaching around from the side, grasp the trigger grips, and in theory walk the tracers onto the target. How two men were to drive the tank and fire three machine guns at the same time never became clear to me. In any event, we only carried weapons when we needed to, and the extra space they left made a big difference when we were inside.

We wore the latest football-helmet style headgear for protection because there was no padding inside the Marmon-Herrington, just a lot of sharp steel interior fittings. We had a great time running around with the vision ports raised, knocking down small trees and churning around the training area. Mattson explained to me why he did each thing, and I began getting the hang of the vehicle. We eventually stopped on top of a steep hill. Bruce asked me if I was ready to take over, but on second thought decided to take it down the steep slope himself. He whipped the tank around, and it promptly began to roll over! My helmet flew off and I grabbed my head to keep it from knocking around. I must not have succeeded, because I woke up in a daze and saw that Mattson was knocked out. He hung upside down relative to my position, and was bleeding profusely from his nose, the blood just pouring on me. I reached over and slapped his cheek. He opened his eyes. I could hear the crackling sound of flames, and yelled, "The tank's on fire what do we do?" Bruce's response was, "We get the hell out of here." I feared that we were trapped inside the upside-down vehicle, but Mattson pointed to the hatch and I saw that it was lying on one side. I was still afraid that we would not get out because it was maybe braced against a tree or something. All of these thoughts occurred in a microsecond, I am sure. I struggled to open the hatch, but could not. Mattson grabbed the handle, gave it a twist, and said, "Get moving!"

I bounded out into grass that was already burning in a ten-foot circle around the vehicle. Looking back, I saw Bruce calmly standing in the flames by the hatch, turning the fire extinguisher handle. He then rather nonchalantly trotted over to me and said, "What are you doing on the ground?" I said I had heard a hissing noise and thought it was going to blow. Bruce shook his head and said that it was the noise made by the fire extinguisher.

The flames continued to flare out of the tank, so we trotted over to the road after fixing Bruce's bloody nose. We caught a ride to the fire station and returned with the fire truck. The fire burned until the tank began to glow cherry red, despite the water poured on it.

A board of investigation convened the next day. They took our statements and those of the platoon sergeant and maintenance sergeant, and then they walked over the ground where we had rolled to determine why the tank had flipped over, why it had caught fire, and why the fire extinguisher had failed to smother the fire. The answers became all too apparent. By following the tank tracks, they discovered a tree stump on the hilltop concealed by grass and surmised that the track had been only partly on the stump, so when Mattson spun around it slipped off and dug under, causing us to flip over. The fire started because of the design of the fuel cap that was a pressure-release type, used because the designer thought the cap should release pressure if the fuel tank was hit by shells. The weight of the fuel overcame the pressure spring, allowing it to spill onto the hot engine. The fire extinguisher did not work because it was designed to cover the engine from the top down with a layer of carbon dioxide foam. However, with the vehicle on its side, the smothering effect was lost.

The investigation board did not find us culpable for the accidental loss of Marine Corps tank number eight (the USMC serial number was simply "T-8"). The report instead faulted the defective design of the fuel cap and fire extinguisher. So ended my first tank ride and Marie's last. I hoped I would never again have to abandon a tank in such circumstances, but it did happen again. Above all, I learned that day that one did not need a war in order to destroy a tank. Marie was the first tank lost by the Marine Corps, but she would not be the last, and I think I made up for her loss with my later service in combat. The Marmon-Herrington tanks all had their fire extinguishers and fuel caps changed as a result of this incident, but it was not possible to provide a second entry or escape hatch. Later tanks, like the M4 Sherman, had good regular and escape hatches, internal fixed fire extinguishers, and portable extinguishers. We often used the latter for cooling Japanese beer.

■　■　■

Most of the 1st Marine Division went to the Caribbean for exercises in the summer of 1941, leaving some units, including my motorcycle platoon, behind at Quantico, probably because of a lack of shipping. It returned to Parris Island in the fall to fill out its new regiments before returning to New River. Units left at Quantico began to move south in October. While the rest of the company was gone, my platoon fell administratively under the commander of the Division Rear Echelon, Col. William G. Hawthorne. During the two months I had to myself, my men and I conducted practice motorcycle reconnaissance missions. We had great fun running all over northern Virginia on our Harley-Davidson WLA cycles, at times using the sidecars. We left the base every day and must have run on every dirt road in the state. It was great for me, running the platoon by myself with a superb platoon sergeant to help. According to Captain Buse, our mission was to reconnoiter the road net in advance of the division, so my training program focused on that: map and aerial photo reading and reporting on what units were at a location, the condition of bridges, and so forth. I was learning my trade.

Not long after the division went off to the Caribbean, Colonel Hawthorne decided to do something for troop morale. He announced that he wanted to hold a cotillion for the enlisted men, and he assigned officers from each of the units that had stayed behind to plan it. I was the junior officer in the rear echelon, and the colonel noted that I had joined the Marine Corps while living in Washington, D.C. He asked me if I could find five hundred girls for the dance, and I, of course, said, "Aye, aye, sir!" One of my former classmates at the University of Maryland had gone to work for the Department of Agriculture. When I called and told him that I needed five hundred girls, he said he could get me five thousand! Thousands of young women had taken jobs in the city, working for the government as typists, punch-card machine operators, receptionists, secretaries, and so forth. They signed up for the dance right away on bulletin boards at Agriculture. The next problem was transportation, so we talked to another former classmate who had gone to work with the Blue-Gray Bus Line and arranged for it to provide ten buses free for the marines.

This all fell into place because Washington had become a very military town even before the war started. I reported to the colonel and he said, "That sounds pretty good, but we still need a motorcycle escort." Yet another former classmate worked for the D.C. police force, so I called him up. The police department agreed to escort the buses to the district line and hand them over to a detachment from the Virginia State Patrol for the rest of the trip to the Quantico gate at Triangle, Virginia. Colonel Hawthorne, who was very impressed and congratulatory, told me that I could escort them the rest of the way on base with my platoon.

We had never operated at night with the motorcycles, and our Harleys had a unique feature that went along with the sidecars: a reverse gear. Muscles Treadwell had taught me to shift with my eyes on the road, doing it by feel. Despite his teaching me this, I always peeked. Now we were lined up in the dark at Triangle Gate for the last eight miles into the base. The buses arrived, with the accompanying State Patrol sirens screaming, and we took off, riding the clutch for a really fast start with engines revved to the maximum. But I had shifted into reverse! I flew forward, my body thrown halfway over the handlebars. The cycle spun around maybe three times. Uncannily, I managed to get the clutch back in and came out of it. The girls cheered at the apparent stunt, but the troops all saw it for what it was and snickered. All the way back to base I was careful not to shift into reverse.

Colonel Hawthorne later invited me to dinner at his house, perhaps reflecting his pleasure in my work. His best friend and Annapolis classmate (and future chief of naval operations) Comdr. Bob Carney, who was stationed at the Naval Academy, was there, too. I was invited as a dinner partner for his daughter. We went for a motorcycle ride and I think she liked it, but it scared her a bit. We corresponded until the beginning of the war and I was beginning to think that I could get serious about her. However, I did not know that she was engaged to a navy officer who was severely wounded at Pearl Harbor. She was not going to leave him. On Iwo Jima, I met her brother, Bob Junior, who served as a platoon leader in the 5th Marine Division in a rifle company commanded by Tom Fields, my buddy from the University of Maryland. A small world, it would seem!

Another job I got because of my junior status involved a boxing smoker for the troops. Heinie Miller, the boxing coach at the University of Maryland, had commanded the Washington, D.C., Marine Corps Reserve battalion and was the 1st Marine Division's real morale officer. We were so close that when he made colonel at New River he had me attend the ceremony to pin on one of his eagles. We put on a great boxing tournament that lasted three or four days. To nobody's surprise, we found great talent among the troops, including many former professionals, Golden Gloves competitors, and fleet boxers.

Rounding out that long, last summer of peace in 1941 was a Hollywood publicity stunt, clearly a scheme of Marine Corps headquarters, that involved six Powers models coming to the base and posing for pictures with our marines. The Powers Agency reigned at the top of the business and so naturally these were good looking babes. A newly commissioned Hollywood-type officer accompanied them as their escort. I do not remember all the details, but one of the things that happened was that they brought the girls to the base swimming pool and took pictures of them with the marines who were there for training. After the shoot was done, they told the guys, "Okay, you can go in if you want." *Whoom!* A hundred guys jumped in the water with those six girls, who likely would have drowned had we not gotten them out. Somewhere I have a picture I got from the publicist of me in a convertible, surrounded by the Powers girls.

Otherwise, life at Quantico consisted of showing up at morning formation, conducting an inspection, and then stating the training problem for the day and executing it with my platoon. Every Saturday night during the summer the officers' club held a dance. We had to wear either a tux or whites. I often found dates for the other lieutenants I knew. It was one of the best summers of my life.

■ ■ ■

When Muscles Treadwell left to become company first sergeant, I had to find a replacement for him. I had two buck sergeants, but they were nowhere near the same class of NCO Muscles had been. I asked Bill Buse if there was somebody else, and he said, "Nobody I know of, but look around and see if there's another sergeant you like in one of the other platoons. If the platoon leader agrees, then you can have him." I had seen Sgt. Mike DeSantis in Gillispie's scout car platoon. I thought he was a pretty snappy sergeant, but Tex, who had a strong prejudice against Mexicans, thought DeSantis was a Chicano. When I told Tex I was interested in having him, Tex told me, "You're damned right you can have him, I don't want any goddamned Mexican in my platoon, anyway." So, for the wrong reason, I got Mike as a platoon sergeant (as it turned out, he was of Italian descent). True to his word, Buse promoted him. Mike DeSantis was one super guy. He was about five years older than me, a ten-year veteran of the Corps, and just a fine NCO.

Soon after moving to join the rest of the 1st Marine Division forming at New River, I found myself detailed as an observer at the army's fall "GHQ Maneuvers" in the Carolinas. The scenario involved the I Armored Corps attacking the rest of the First Army. First Lieutenant Ray Schwenke and I were assigned to an army mechanized cavalry regiment, which operated in a way most similar to our own scout company. It was a National Guard outfit from Philadelphia, known as the "Blue Stocking Troop," an old-time social and political guard unit. The officers were all Philadelphia Main Line social types, and the colonel commanding the regiment edited or published one of the city's papers. He had a studied British look, with a tall and commanding presence about him. It had originally been a "portee" horse cavalry squadron, which consisted of horses carried in trucks from which they would mount and carry out regular cavalry missions. After being federalized, the regiment had been enlarged with a battalion of tanks. The theory was that the horses would scout and the tanks exploit. Although the enlisted tankers were blue-collar types from the Bronx and could not match the officers socially, they accepted the regiment's customs in good old-fashioned American style, and all wore spurs and boots in their tanks. The regiment's motto was "Over, under, or through!" and the guys from the Bronx would say, "Yeah: overworked, underpaid, and never through!"

We were attached to these troops for two weeks. The colonel would call in his senior officers at the end of each of day to one of the portee wagons outfitted as a bar for a drink and to critique operations. He always invited Schwenke and me, a first and second lieutenant, out of respect for "regulars." One evening, the colonel told a story about a British cavalry regiment that had been badly shot up in the 1940 campaign. Most of its men had escaped through Dunkirk, but without their horses, and later reassembled in England, where the regimental commander told his officers that they were being transferred to tanks in order to satisfy the army's needs. Their motto, "love and gallop," had existed for hundreds of years, but now he told them: "I'd think it appropriate to get a new motto with the same spirit but more appropriate to these iron monsters. Please think it over and propose it next month." The great day came, and a subaltern spoke up from the rear of the club, telling the colonel that he thought he had one that would fit his desires for a motto appropriate to the regiment but reflecting the new times. "Well," the colonel replied, "what is it, my boy?" To which the subaltern replied, "Instead of 'love and gallop,' I propose, 'screw and bolt'." I usually do not remember jokes very long, but that one has stuck with me for more than sixty years.

During those maneuvers, I got a glimpse of General Patton, who was then commanding the 2d Armored Division. We had a lot of shortages and the army was using trucks marked "tank" and broomsticks marked "antitank," but Patton had real tanks. There was a long road trestle crossing a canyon, and our armored cavalry regiment had the job of defending the site. We set up machine guns, antitank broom handles, and other "weapons" to cover the road. Sure enough, we soon heard the rumble of tanks. We looked out from a wooded area; there was no room for the tanks to maneuver. Schwenke and I saw them cross the bridge and start down the road. General Patton stood waist high in the turret of the lead tank, his pistols in shoulder holsters, looking bigger than life. His tanks followed nose to tail behind him, with no dispersion or anything tactical about them. At that moment, an umpire ran up to him with his flag, shouting: "General! General! You're all knocked out!" Patton looked down at the man and said, "Listen you SOB, I'm going to give you three seconds to get out of the way or you'll be mincemeat," and then on they went, out of range.

We did not learn much from the maneuvers, except that the army was very unprepared for fighting, and that we were doing much better.

We spent the last night at a hotel in Columbia, South Carolina, and that was like heaven.

Life at New River remained much simpler than at Quantico, for we lived in tent cities and had few social distractions. We were not at war, and the division had deployed to Cuba and made several landings at Culebra Island. We were now a seventy-five-thousand-man Marine Corps, and we were amazed at what was going on. We had a number of interesting encounters with civilians on our reconnaissance exercises. The people in the coastal area of North Carolina were very poor and had little education. There were few roads, and only the one to Wilmington was paved. Most of the locals probably had never seen a motorcycle.

As an example, the division staged a large-scale maneuver in late November, starting with landings at Onslow Beach, and then advancing inland. We were the advance guard doing a route reconnaissance. The opposition consisted of the 1st Marine Aircraft Wing and the 1st Parachute Battalion. We ran about checking the bridges, scouting for the paratroopers, and watching out for enemy planes. We took no sidecars because the roads were so rough and narrow, so the second rider rode behind the driver, watching his sector for aircraft as each squad moved along the route. All of a sudden, the guy behind me pointed out three aircraft, flying slow and noisy. I saw from an aerial photo we were using that we were approaching a village, and figured we could hide there. I gave the signal to go full speed and headed there. We hit the sandy crossroads and there was the village, complete with general store, with a mule and buckboard tied up and people sitting on the porch. We all went into a sliding stop, sending the sand and dust into the air. Several "enemy" aircraft had also arrived, so I commanded: "Planes! Scatter! Take cover!" The men knew exactly what to do. The planes dived on us and the civilians ran inside their houses in terror. The planes dropped flour bags all around, but hit none of us.

The civilians were very shaken by the whole episode. "All clear, assemble here," I called out. From inside the store came a little voice, "Does he mean us, Mummie?" I realized that we must look like men from Mars to these people, dressed as we were in motorcycle coveralls, ski masks, and helmets, and carrying tommy guns. I ran up the steps, knocked on the door, and said: "Please come out, we're friends. We're U.S. Marines on maneuvers!" After a while they came out, and I explained what we were doing. We stayed to have a Coca-Cola, and then left. I even took the owner of the mule and buckboard down the road to catch up with them, as the mule had bolted during all the commotion.

■ ■ ■

The 1st Marine Division commander, Maj. Gen. Alexander A. Vandegrift, authorized a ninety-six-hour pass for everybody after the maneuver and offered his congratulations. Half the division would go that weekend and half the next. A lot of guys did not want to go right away because they had made no plans, but I knew instinctively not to turn down liberty at the first opportunity. Tex and I went to Raleigh and met two girls we knew from Richmond who had come down on the train. After a very busy weekend, we went to a Sunday afternoon matinee before our dates had to catch their train. We sat through the movie in a theater full of marines. At the end, a civilian walked out on the stage and announced that Japan and the United States were at war. After a moment of silence, all the guys threw their hats in the air and cheered. We began singing the "Marine's Hymn." I was shaking with excitement. I remember thinking that if the Japanese could have seen the reaction they had prompted, they would regret what they had done.

We took the girls to the station and learned more while listening to the radio on the way back to camp. Pearl Harbor and the Philippines both had been attacked. We were at war. The other guys in the division did not get to go on their ninety-six-hour liberty, after all. The attitude expressed at the first company formation the next day was prevalent throughout the United States. Captain Buse gave us a wonderful pep talk, concluding, "By God, if we have to go to war, there's no one we'd rather fight than those little slant-eyed bastards!" We cheered wildly.

When I made first lieutenant at New River, in April, 1942, the 1st Tank Battalion commander, Maj. Griff Meints, wanted me to be the executive officer of the new D Company that he had to form. I felt that Mike DeSantis should have the motorcycle platoon as he worked very well. He was a junior college graduate who had enlisted and Buse agreed to give him a field commission. He took over the platoon, and later commanded the company at Peleliu. He sent for his girlfriend from the Bronx, and they were married the day he got his commission. I was best man. Years later he retired as a lieutenant colonel.

Meints proved to be a big disappointment. We first met when the scout company joined the 1st Tank Battalion. My first real conversation I had with him came when I was the battalion duty officer and we had to send a firefighting detail to help put out a blaze in the nearby forest.

Meints came out and complemented me on how I was running the detail. Later on, in 1942, when I made captain, he sent me away to the Training Command instead of another captain. He should have sent somebody who had been on Guadalcanal, but I guess by then he just wanted to get rid of me. In the end, I was not unhappy to return to the United States after doing nothing in New Zealand, but what I really wanted was a tank company.

With our entry into the war, the Corps did a very smart thing. All marine gunners (warrant officers) were promoted to first lieutenant, and all chief warrant officers to captain. Edgar C. "Dusty" Hughes, our old, hard-drinking, salty, bar ordnance officer, thus became a first lieutenant. He immediately asked Griff Meints for permission to hold saluting school for the second lieutenants and, amazingly, Meints gave it. So Dusty, who apparently had suffered much chagrin from watching the new young gentlemen strut around, had the last word. I roomed with Dusty, and it was he who suggested to me that Meints hated lieutenants first, and me second.

The promotion of many of us to first lieutenant led to a near debacle in our finances. The raise was a healthy one, about $40 (from $120 per month), and we pooled our money to throw one hell of a "wetting-down" party for all of the battalion's officers. Then the word came down that for the duration of the war, officers would receive no subsistence pay for housing, in order to show solidarity with the forces in the field and in action and living under primitive shelter, if any. That more than devoured the raise, and many of us almost went into hock with the promotion as a result.[2]

New deployments began after Pearl Harbor. The 7th Marines was ordered to reinforce Samoa.[3] Just as the prewar Iceland brigade from the 2d Marine Division (then without a scout company) had taken Reed Fawell, our executive officer, with detachments from the scout company—a platoon of scout cars and a squad from the motorcycle platoon—so this new 3d Brigade took another slice from the platoon, as well as our new C Company, 1st Tank Battalion, under Capt. Rowland Hall. The rest of the division prepared to move by rail to San Francisco and then to sail to the South Pacific. I had one last liberty in Washington, and was stricken with appendicitis. They did an excellent operation on me at Bethesda Naval Hospital and I convinced the surgeon that I just had to be on my way. I wired both Captain Buse and General Vandegrift and pleaded with them to take me along, on straggler's orders if necessary. The trains were already loading and heading west by then. My telegram apparently impressed the general enough that he authorized an airline ticket to allow me to catch up. I called my parents and we had a very quiet dinner together at the airport in Washington the night that I flew. I did not know if I would ever see them again and it was a very poignant evening.

Once in the airplane, a standard DC-3 airliner with twenty-one seats, I saw that a very stunning stewardess was attending us and I lost all notion of sentimentality. I was traveling in uniform, of course, and when I told her that I was heading for the Pacific and convalescing from an operation, she became very attentive. I told her that it was also my first flight and that I was a bit worried. She told me that flying was easy, but that if it would make me feel better, she would sit beside me on the armrest. Sure enough, after we took off she sat down and held my arm all the way to the first stop, which, I believe, was Nashville, Tennessee. I was flying very high, as they say, and thought that this would be a fine cross-country trip. However, when we left the airplane for refueling, I was stunned to see "my" stewardess dressed in an overcoat and another, very frumpy stewardess getting ready to board. They quickly explained to me that the first girl was at the end of her day, but that the new one would be glad to take care of me for the rest of the trip. After we took off again, I assured the new girl that I was feeling fine and thanked her for her concern.

My convalescent status paid off one more time, as I was able to escape the shellback treatment when we crossed the equator. I rode the liner MV *Kungsholm*, the flagship of the Swedish Lines, and she was still in her prewar condition. We had sumptuous quarters and fine food for the trip "down under" to Wellington, New Zealand. There we expected to train the 1st and 2d Marine Divisions for the eventual Allied offensive against the Japanese, supposedly set to begin in 1943.

CHAPTER 4

Early Tests in the Southwest Pacific

We began to unload the 1st Tank Battalion from our transports at Wellington in July, 1942, and made an administrative and training camp at Petone Beach. But already plans had changed for us. A limited offensive was already in the planning stage as the division crossed the Pacific in various convoys. The alarming spread of Japanese detachments south and east of Rabaul on New Britain in the Solomons threatened the vital sea-lanes supporting Australia and the bases from which the Southwest Pacific Area (SWPA) command planned to launch its campaign to recover the Philippines. Pacific Fleet forces would land the 1st Marine Division on Guadalcanal and Tulagi to take the Japanese air and seaplane bases there in an effort to block any further advance. The islands thus seized would later serve as jumping-off bases for the planned reduction of Japanese positions at Rabaul and the northern coast of New Guinea.[1]

Shipping and reinforcements in the theater proved scarce for Operation Watchtower, the amphibious landing's code name, and the 2d Marines with attached supporting companies finally joined the division after sailing directly from Camp Elliott in the United States. The shipping shortages and hurried reloading at Wellington contributed to a disheartening rehearsal landing exercise in the Fiji Islands, whence the task forces headed for the objective area. Only the 1st Tank Battalion's A and B Companies and the 2d Tank Battalion's C Company (with the 2d Marines) would go with the assault troops. The 1st Tank Battalion's headquarters remained at Petone Beach with its Headquarters Company and D Company. Vandegrift left most of his motor transport behind as well, so the 1st Scout Company remained, too.

The New Zealand dockworkers did not help us at all as we struggled to off-load the transports and then reload them for an amphibious assault. It rained every day, and the dockhands' contract said they could not be forced to work in the rain, so their shop stewards enforced the union rules. They later complained that they had no idea a major offensive was in the works, but we could not tell anyone that for fear of creating a security leak. Those of us left behind at Wellington assumed that we would also go up to Guadalcanal on follow-on shipping, but this never materialized and the campaign turned into a desperate air and naval battle to keep what we had on Guadalcanal properly supplied and alive, let alone reinforced.

Griff Meints stayed behind when our two tank companies went to Guadalcanal (the third one was on Samoa with the 7th Marines). Little leadership skill was required for running the battalion headquarters in Wellington. Looking back, I think that perhaps he was not much of a leader. He had no concept of tank-infantry tactics, although he knew how to run a battalion in garrison. Maybe Vandegrift did not want him on Guadalcanal. We later learned that the tanks had few chances for combat and Vandegrift, under the existing doctrine, made his weapons battalion commander, Lt. Col. Bob Luckey, the antitank officer.

Meints finally transferred me to D Company on August 7, and I worked for Capt. Donald J. Robinson for about a month. Robinson had been one of the first tankers, back in the days of the old 1st Tank Company at Quantico, and he gave me a free hand in supervising the training of this very green outfit. The scout company left the battalion in September to serve as a separate company, the way it was when I joined it. Tex Gillespie went to Guadalcanal with Harvey "Wally" Walseth's A Company and was wounded there. He received a medical discharge.

Tom O'Mahoney (pronounced "O-Manney"), took command of the scout company and carried out the orders to reform it as a foot- and jeep-mobile outfit for the rest of the war. He was one of the four second lieutenants from the 5th ROC who joined the 1st Scout Company when it entered the Fleet Marine Force (FMF). By the time my ex-platoon sergeant Mike DeSantis took command before the Peleliu assault, it was simply the division reconnaissance company. Tom later married a great gal in Australia. *Life* magazine had an issue in 1943 about Australian war brides, a cover story, as I recall. Among the twenty-five thumbnail photos and paragraphs on each couple, she stood out as one gorgeous girl. I saw Tom once after the war, when I was in the inactive reserve. I was walking on the street near an apartment I lived in on Wilshire Boulevard and saw a Marine Corps major cross the street. It was Tom. He was an officer-instructor in the University of California Los Angeles navy ROTC unit and was on his way to another duty station. We had a great impromptu reunion there in Westwood.

I was back in tanks with D Company, and we trained every day in our new fourteen-ton M3 light tanks. These were real tanks compared to Marie and her sisters in the old scout company. We later graduated to brand-new M5s at Jacque's Farm. The M3 light tank had increased frontal armor for the hull (1.75 inches thick) and turret (1.5-inch gun shield). The main armament was a 37-mm antitank gun, mounted in the turret. A shoulder yoke allowed the gunner to make limited traverse and elevation adjustments, and a manual turret traverse mechanism provided full 360-degree turret rotation. The M3A1 version featured a power traverse turret with a turret basket and two-inch gun-shield armor. A vertical gyrostabilizer unit was added to production vehicles, but I never saw any of these. A modified aircraft engine, a 262-horsepower Continental radial, powered this little tank, which literally flew at thirty-six miles per hour—and even faster if we disconnected the governor.

We practiced driving unbuttoned and buttoned up in a mile-square training area outside of Wellington. One day, Mike DeSantis and I had a few drinks in a local pub and met some Royal New Zealand Air Force (RNZAF) guys who were home on leave from North Africa. They wanted to know what we did, and when we told them we were with a tank unit, we struck a deal for them to train with us. So they flew some air support for us and we practiced attacking after air strikes. They went back to North Africa afterward.

I still have a scar from one of those training days. The field had a five-yard deep ditch on one side that was too narrow to pass through and too wide to jump, but one day I decided to try. It was cold and I wore gloves. We made it to the other side but really landed hard. My left hand flew off the steering lever and banged against the interior of the hull. It hurt like hell, but I thought nothing of it in the excitement of making the jump. Later, when we got back to camp and started to clean up, I took off the glove and blood spilled out of it. I had split a finger just from the impact. That was my most memorable field training experience in New Zealand.

■ ■ ■

We continued to live on the MV *Kungsholm* for many days after our arrival, and on one of these a young New Zealander dressed in civilian clothes came aboard looking for a "Leftenant" Neiman. It turned out that he represented the Wellington Fencing Club, which was hosting the All–New Zealand Saber Finals. He wanted to invite me to participate, having somehow learned from the U.S. Fencing Association that I was an officer in the 1st Marine Division. I told him that I was not exactly in training form for saber competition, but he assured me that most New Zealand men between the ages of twenty and forty were in North Africa with the army and I would only be fencing old men and young boys.

I accompanied the young man to the Wellington Fencing Club and watched several men practicing in the loft. He was right: most of the competition would be below my normal level. However, there was one man, a bit older than I, who looked pretty good as he practiced with the saber. When I asked about him, my host told me that he was a Hungarian army officer who had been interned in New Zealand, but was granted permission to compete in the tournament.

My host introduced us, and I soon became good friends with Col. George Kerekes, who was indeed an engineer in the Hungarian army. It turned out that he was a leader in the anti-German faction of their army and had to flee Adm. Miklós Horthy's goon squads in 1941, traveling with his wife, Zlata, and young daughter by train to Istanbul and then by ship to Shanghai. George had visited San Francisco to observe the construction of the Golden Gate Bridge in the 1930s and intended to take his wife and eight-year-old daughter there as émigrés. But the Pearl Harbor attack took place when they were in midocean, and his British passenger ship had diverted to the nearest safe haven—New Zealand. By then, Hungary was in the war on Germany's side and George found himself interned. The New Zealand government welcomed him, however, and at the time we met he was working for them as an engineer. We competed in the tournament finals, which he won five to four after a close match.

I enjoyed many evenings with George and his family and even managed to renew our friendship after the war. I was competing in the Pacific Coast Fencing Tournament in 1947, with the Los Angeles Athletic Club and I decided to check the local telephone book to see if George and Zlata had ever made it to the United States, figuring that he would have settled in the Bay Area. And there was his name, the only Kerekes in the book. We had a fine talk and he came to see me fence the next day, spiriting me home for dinner and an overnight stay afterward. After that I visited them whenever I returned to San Francisco on business.

While still in New Zealand, I saw my first prisoners of war: Korean laborers who had been sent back from Guadalcanal. Very few Japanese surrendered during the war, and most of those who did were wounded. The troops bringing them back had taught them a few songs and, to my surprise, they came down the gangway at Wellington singing "God Bless America" in unison. The things one sees in a war!

■ ■ ■

I had a nice girlfriend in Wellington. Her name was Noni Gillis, and she was the advertising manager for one of the large D.I.C. department stores. The store occupied a five- or six-story building, and she lived in a roof bungalow above it. I saw her every night after George Kerekes and his wife introduced us. We corresponded after I left New Zealand and I felt that I would be back some day. Years later she married a New Zealand submarine officer. We continued to correspond even though we were both married. She named her first child Robert, but that was also her husband's first name.

The coming of the war changed sexual mores and attitudes in America, of course, and these took on the notion of "here today, gone tomorrow," so to speak. Even so, they never quite reached the level we saw with the New Zealand girls. In the first place, the gals in New Zealand told us that they had not had an able-bodied man around for several years. Apparently New Zealand had contributed more men per capita to its armed forces than any other nation. Nearly all the men aged seventeen to forty had gone away to fight, so the girls in 1942 reportedly were waiting on the hills with field glasses, watching for the arrival of U.S. ships crammed with thousands of young men. It was really nice.

We marines found out, much to our pleasure—although it was not so with Noni—that if a New Zealand girl liked you enough to make a date, then she also liked you well enough to go to bed with you. We, on the other hand, had been brought up to believe that "nice girls" did not do that until they got married, and that most of the girls who would go to bed with you would not do it on the first date. You thus had to try your darnedest to convince them that you were the kind of guy they wanted to have a sexual relationship with, and it might take quite a while. But in New Zealand, often on the first date, but rarely later than the second date, marines found that they were ready to go.

I had a most interesting experience in this aspect. After arriving on MV *Kundsholm*, it seemed that in no time at all several officers of the tank battalion had some girls lined up. I found myself with a girl we will call "Millie." One night I took Millie on a date to the Saint George Hotel. Not long after arriving, the hotel began to shake, and I thought, "This is a hell of a party," but then I realized that it was an earthquake! Millie started screaming, and the plaster began falling from the ceiling. We ran out of the building, and the date came to a sudden conclusion. That was my first earthquake and a brief first encounter with a Kiwi girl.

Noni and I enjoyed being together, but we never went "all the way." Had I remained in New Zealand, I probably would have gotten engaged just like Tom O'Mahoney and his Aussie. So that was the way it was in New Zealand for the most part. The first or second date, a New Zealand girl would go to bed with you. We were mostly young kids, and life then was wonderful—the average age in the scout company, including the officers and NCOs, was 19.5 years, although I turned 24 before leaving. Previously, in the United States, I had enjoyed lots of dates and already considered myself a man of the world, but I never imagined a social life like the one we had in New Zealand.

■　■　■

I had my only experience with a prisoner detail while I was in New Zealand. A number of marines had gone AWOL and missed shipping out for Guadalcanal because they had shacked up with New Zealand girls, not because they were afraid to fight with the division. The military police (MPs) had rounded up about twenty-five such men, and I took charge of the detail assigned to take them by train to Auckland, New Zealand's largest city, located on the northern tip of North Island. From there they were to be taken to Guadalcanal by ship. Three gunnery sergeants made up my guard detail, and all of us were armed with Thompson submachine guns. We lined the prisoners up outside of the Cecil

Hotel, which had served as division headquarters in Wellington, and now functioned as the rear echelon headquarters. The three gunnies faced them, guns held at the ready, and I had my tommy gun slung over my shoulder. I was really angry with these guys and told them so. I said I hoped some of them would try to escape because nothing would give me more pleasure than shooting them. "How do you gunnies feel?" I asked the NCOs. "Same way!" they growled.

We marched to the train station and boarded a car reserved for us on the nightly sleeper train. There were no dining cars, so we had to stop en route for meals. We let the men get off, but guarded them closely. The New Zealand people could not understand it. They saw marines as gods sent to protect them, not as prisoners under guard, and we had to tell them to stay away. The next day, we delivered our charges to a merchantman chartered for carrying supplies to Guadalcanal. It seemed that one of the deserters was a hard case, a true dissenter. The rest were chagrined to be considered deserters and wanted to rejoin their outfits, after having had their fun in Wellington. Later, on Guadalcanal, I learned that they had beat the hell out of the one guy aboard ship and wanted to throw him overboard. The ship's captain had to intervene to save him.

I was walking along Queen's Street the next afternoon, killing time before our train's scheduled departure for Wellington, and happened to find a Boot's Pharmacy store—a common British chain. I needed razor blades, so I entered it. Inside, I saw the cutest blonde girl behind the counter. I struck up a conversation with her. It was 4:30 and I started kidding around with her. I pulled the train ticket from my pocket and said, "I have to go back to Wellington tonight on the train, but tell me, if I didn't have to go back, would you have had dinner with me?" I was enjoying this flirting. "Why, yes," she replied, "it would be a pleasure to go out to dinner with you."

On my way back to the station, I ran into Lt. Col. Eugene Collier, who had been Colonel Hawthorne's executive officer in the Division Special Troops back at Quantico. I had not seen him since, and we had a nice reunion on the street. He asked me what I was doing there, so I told him. "You don't want to ride that old rickety train back," he said. "Why don't you fly with me in the morning; I have the general's plane." Vandegrift had one of those twin-tailed Beechcraft planes on Guadalcanal and Collier had left there on a mission to the Rear Echelon. He told me to be at the airport in the morning. I dashed to the railroad station and cashed in my ticket, then went on to Boot's Pharmacy and convinced the girl to stick by her word and go out for dinner. She told me she knew a nice place, but she said we would need a car and pointed out a car rental outfit. The cars operated on charcoal boilers that made coal gas to power the engines. It was the first British car I had driven, and it was quite a contraption—tall and narrow, driver on the right side—but we managed to get to the place she wanted.

It was a converted old country farmhouse, remodeled so that one entered a living room with a big fireplace. The room served as a cocktail lounge. The proprietor asked us to order in advance and we did so. He invited us to have a drink and said dinner would be served upstairs. That sounded pretty curious to me. After finishing our drinks we went up and were ushered into a lovely bedroom. It had a fireplace with two loveseats placed in front and a coffee table set for two. There was also a bed and a few other pieces of furniture. The dinner was very nice—not mutton—the best I ate in New Zealand. We spent the whole evening there and, come morning, had to make a mad dash back to the car rental office. We parted company there. She went back to Boot's and I headed for the airport.

On the way back with Lieutenant Colonel Collier, I saw the spectacular Mount Egmont, located halfway south on the island's western shore, standing on its own peninsula. It has an even more perfect cone than Mount Fuji, and it appeared to rise out of the ocean as we flew south along the coastline. After landing at Wellington, I reported mission accomplished to the Division Rear Echelon.

I had another strange experience while serving as the tank battalion officer of the day in Wellington. We had a holding brig for minor offenders in the battalion. One day, when we had the old battalion troublemaker in it (every battalion had at least one such perpetual offender), one of my old motorcycle troops from the scout company, a little guy, was on guard and he asked me: "What do I do if this SOB comes at me? He's been threatening to get me when he's released from the brig." I said something like, "Is your rifle loaded?" He said it was or could be, and I said: "Well, just shoot him, but in the leg. Don't shoot to kill, just shoot to stop him—and be sure to warn him."

Later in the day, sure enough, that is exactly what happened. The guy was released and came after him. The guard did exactly what I said, calling out, "Halt, or I'll shoot!" The guy did not believe him, so the guard shot him in the leg, dropping him. That ended the incident.

■   ■   ■

I celebrated my twenty-fourth birthday in Wellington, but already my days there were numbered. The Marine Corps had promoted me to captain that day, backdated to August 7, the date of the Guadalcanal landing. Because of the way we had all entered the service together, we now had far too many captains for the few jobs available. Meints made me his battalion intelligence officer (S2) on the fourth, and when he later received word that he would have to transfer a captain back to the states to the training command, he undoubtedly saw a way to get rid of me. With nothing to do in New Zealand, I was not unhappy about returning to the United States, but I would have preferred to take command of a tank company.

I left New Zealand in early October. Some other 1st Marine Division officers transferred later to the states for the training command and new organizations, including some men right off of Guadalcanal. Many of them flew back, but I embarked on a navy cargo ship bound for San Francisco. Although this was no MV *Kungsholm*, I had a special status, since I outranked the six officers on board except the captain, a lieutenant commander, and was the sole passenger. The ship went first to Auckland, but then received orders to take urgent cargo to Guadalcanal. We sailed alone into waters considered too dangerous for a convoy.

When we arrived, I asked the skipper how long we would be there. He figured it would take three days to unload. I decided to go ashore to talk to the tankers who had fought there and take some of their experiences back with me to the training command. The island lay just a few thousand yards from our ship: black, ominous, and swarming with marines. There was no sign of the Japanese. Walking around Henderson Field, I passed lots of wrecked and some serviceable planes, and saw lots of bomb and shell craters. I found the tanks there, and ran into Leo Case, a tank platoon leader and personal friend, and he told me what was going on.

I knew nothing at that point of the battle on the Tenaru River where Leo had fought. He described the fight against a Japanese special battalion that had entered a coconut palm grove, with hundreds of palms in rows, little cover, and almost no brush. They were trapped, with the ocean on one side, and the 1st Marines on the other. Apparently Leo was jumping to get in and Col. Clifton Cates finally let him go. Leo said it was a field day, as the Japanese had no antitank weapons. He spent an hour running over them with his five M2A4 light tanks (an early version of our M3s), firing 37-mm canister rounds and machine guns. One Japanese infantryman stopped a tank by jamming a bogey wheel with his rifle, disabling it. Leo moved one tank in at a time and had it open a hatch and take a man into the good tank, while the other three circled around providing protection. They repeated this sequence until all four of the crewmen in the stalled tank were out. Leo had taken no casualties, so they continued in action. Cates finally called him on the radio and instructed him to pull back. "I'm too busy killing Japs!" Leo replied, and stayed there. He was that kind of a guy. Cates took it okay and did not court-martial him. He later recommended Leo for the Navy Cross, which he got. Leo told me the main problem he experienced in the campaign was defending against night infiltrators that frequently passed through the infantry and came upon the tanks, which were stationed near the airfield in reserve.

The only enemy I saw was "Washing Machine Charlie," a Japanese bomber that flew overhead at night, dropping flares and a few desultory bombs. One night, a cruiser shelled Henderson Field. The shells fell randomly and caused little damage. It was my first experience under fire, but all I could do was sit in my hole and ride it out. We finally reboarded the ship and, much to my surprise, cruised back to Wellington. I had already said good-bye to the battalion and here I was returning after only three weeks, still very far from San Francisco. I had a few days of fun ashore and continued to live on the ship. I saw Mike DeSantis for the last time during the war, and then we finally weighed anchor for the United States.

I arrived in San Francisco in early November, 1942. At that point, I was one of the first Southwest Pacific veterans to return from the combat zone, especially Guadalcanal. I knew my orders specified six days delay en route and I had heard all these marvelous stories from the guys. The 1st Marine Division had arrived in San Francisco by train on its way to the war and had become the toast of the town, so I had thought and dreamed about doing the same. I walked down the gangplank and flagged a taxi. Of course, me being a brand-new captain of marines, I was really feeling my oats. Like a big shot, I said, "Take me to the best hotel in town." He said: "Will the Saint Francis do? Its right on the Square." I told him that would be fine.

When the taxi pulled up in front of the Saint Francis, I bounded up the stairs to the front doors, where a big doorman stood. I could see through the windows that a huge crowd had gathered around the front desk, and I wondered what had happened. Was there a robbery? Had someone had a heart attack? The last time I had been in a hotel in the states, they were begging us to go in, so when I asked the doorman what was going on, I was surprised when he replied: "Oh, its all those servicemen coming into town for the weekend, but we don't have any rooms. You have a reservation don't you?" I said no, and elbowed myself forward to the desk, afraid that my dream was about to be shattered. I got to the clerk, whose head was about to come off from shaking it—no, no, no—in response to the repeated pleas of the crowd. "What do you want, captain?" he asked. I told him I wanted a room and he said, "I don't have any." I reached across the desk and grabbed him by his shirt, and said, "Listen you SOB, I've just come back from Guadalcanal and I've been sleeping in a foxhole and I want to sleep in a bed in the Saint Francis Hotel." As soon as I said that, his face changed immediately. "How long will you be staying with us, captain?" he asked. I told him about six days. When I let him go, he said, "Let's see what I can do." He returned a few minutes later and said, "Well, if you would not mind taking a sample room for the weekend, on Monday, we'll put you in a regular room for the remainder of your stay."

I had no idea what a sample room was, but I took it. It turned out to be the largest hotel room I have ever seen, with a row of sofas along one side. Sample rooms, I soon learned, were used by traveling salesmen, who would stay and display their wares in the same room. After showing me into this very large, strange room, the bellman pulled down a double Murphy bed. That was fine by me. I showered, put on a clean uniform, and went to the bar for a drink.

At last I was in the city of my dreams. I entered a long cocktail lounge, with a bar on one side, booths down the other, and some small tables in the middle. About halfway down, I spotted a navy officer from the ship I had just departed. I went over and he invited me to sit with him. He told me that he was married, lived in San Diego, and at the moment was waiting for a call to get through to his wife. As we drank, three or four young ladies come in and sat down at a booth together. One of them was a real knockout. I must have had something of a gleam in my eye, I guess. "You see that good-looking babe?" I asked. "I'm going to have dinner with her tonight!" He replied, "You're out of your mind." Meantime, his call arrived and he left. As he went out, a Marine Corps lieutenant came in with a girl who turned out to be his wife. They stopped at the girls' table and talked briefly, then sat down at the table next to mine.

I went over immediately, introduced myself to them, and said: "You obviously know that young lady. Would you introduce me?" The lieutenant grinned and replied, "Whenever you're ready, captain!" I finished my martini, relishing the moment. The girl who had caught my eye kept smiling at me. I could not stand it anymore and told the lieutenant to take me over there. After the lieutenant had introduced us— her name was Patsy Griffin—she said, "Captain, if the lieutenant had not brought you over to my table, I was going to yours." Holy mackerel! I could not believe my good luck. We immediately agreed to dinner and I said, "Let's have a drink at my table before we go." The navy officer returned from his call after we had placed out order, and I introduced Patsy and told him we were going to dinner. He could not believe it.

I had no idea where to go, and Patsy said: "Well, there's a very romantic restaurant on top of Telegraph Hill called 'The Shadow.' It's all candlelight with a view of the bay and the food is very good." We got a cab and went up on the hill, where we indeed had a very romantic dinner. I was just in heaven. After we ate, we decided to go dancing. During the 1930s there was a popular dance band led by Ted Fiorito. One night a week he broadcast a radio show from the top-story lounge of the Mark Hopkins Hotel on Nob Hill. "Let's go to the 'Top of the Mark,'" I said. "Ted Fiorito plays there." She said: "You're wrong, he actually plays at the 'Bottom of the Mark.' Only tourists go to the 'Top of the Mark.'" So we went there, and while we were there I placed a call to my parents in New York City.

Patsy was a good dancer and we were having a lot of fun, but the "witching hour" was approaching, and I was anticipating even more fun. Finally she looked at me and said, "I suppose you're wondering why I was so anxious to meet you." I replied that I supposed it was because of my good looks or some stupid thing like that, and she said, "Read this, I just got it today." It was a letter written to her by a good friend of mine in the 1st Marine Division on Guadalcanal. He wrote that a number of new captains would be flying back to the states for a variety of reasons and they should be arriving about the time his letter got there. "Why don't you stop the first one you see and find out if he's just off Guadalcanal and able to tell you how I am?" he continued. It turns out I was the first such captain she had seen back in the bar at the Saint Francis. The guy was her fiancé, and I knew him, so I told her that he was fine and so forth.

It became a very platonic date at that point, however, and I got a cab and took her back to her parents' house, where she was staying. I kissed her gently on the cheek and said goodnight and that ended that. I got out of the cab at the hotel and took a walk to cool off. I saw the Drake Hotel and recalled hearing some 1st Marine Division guys say it was a great place to pick up girls. I went inside and there at a table were two new captains from the 1st Parachute Battalion, both of whom I knew very well. They had left Guadalcanal later, but by air, I soon found out. They were sitting with three girls, one of whom they handed over to me, and we had a nice reunion. The party went on through the night.

That was my first night in San Francisco. On Monday, I went to the personnel office, received my train ticket, and drew an advance on my pay. The next day, I noticed that the rate posted for the room, printed on a card inside a closet door, was $36 a night. No wonder the clerk had asked me if I would mind taking a sample room. Here it was Tuesday already, and I was going to be broke soon! I stormed down to the desk. Fortunately, the same clerk was on duty. I asked why he had not moved me to another room on Monday as promised and he looked at me as if I had just stabbed him in the back. "Why, captain, what's the matter with the sample room?" I told him, and he replied, "Well don't worry, we are only charging you $6 a night." So ended my first visit to the city by the bay, which has forever charmed me—as have a lot of things about California life.

CHAPTER 5

Training Command

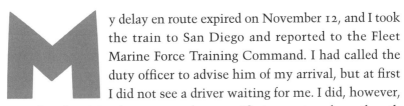

My delay en route expired on November 12, and I took the train to San Diego and reported to the Fleet Marine Force Training Command. I had called the duty officer to advise him of my arrival, but at first I did not see a driver waiting for me. I did, however, see Col. Robert Hogaboom, one of our terrific instructors from the 4th ROC at Quantico. I walked over to say hello. It turned out that he was the Training Command operations officer. Hogaboom wanted to talk about my future assignments, so we went to the station coffee shop. His primary concern was a letter I had written to headquarters from New Zealand, requesting a transfer to Marine Corps aviation and pilot training. I had been pretty fed up with sitting around New Zealand and saw this as a way to get into the war, especially since Griff Meints remained unlikely to give me a shot at command. Hogaboom probably thought that headquarters would approve the transfer, since we were creating new air wings and separate squadrons as fast as we were divisions in those days. They probably approved anybody who could pass the flight physical. It turns out Hogaboom wanted me for the tank school being formed at Camp Elliott, the home of the Training Command, on the northern outskirts of San Diego. If he lost me to flight school, there would be more delays while he waited for another tank captain to be sent back from overseas.

When I confided to him that what I really wanted was command of a tank company, he seemed relieved and made me the following offer, which I still suspect was rather unique. He said that if I agreed to retract my letter requesting aviation and take the assignment to Camp Elliott, he could guarantee that I would be given command of the next tank company formed on the West Coast. He told me up front that none would be forming for several months, but he also told me that as the tank school operations officer I would be able to handpick the officers and men for the new company. He even told me that I would be able to hold promising personnel over as additional instructors, in order to have them available for the new company. The offer seemed too good to be true, but I knew Hogaboom was a totally reliable officer, so I agreed to his terms. Why did he do it? I suppose he must have been impressed that I wanted a command badly, and he knew that I would work like the devil at the school for this "reward." These perceptive powers proved he was another of those top-notch officers we had in the ROC in 1941. He retired years later as a four-star general.

Hogaboom passed word of the deal on to my new boss, Maj. William R. "Rip" Collins, who ran the Tank School, FMF Training Center, as it was then called. Much to my amazement, he never questioned any of this. The school was brand-new, having just been formed in July by Collins. It was the answer to the terrible problems we had encountered with expanding the Marine Corps and preparing tank units for war in so little time. Rip had served as Meints's executive officer in the 1st Tank Company and also served as the tank officer on the Marine Corps Equipment Board in 1940. For the next two years, he and the tank school's instructor staff would train marines to operate and maintain the various tank types and models we cycled through during the war.

Camp Elliot had already been expanded with the purchase of more land, and we had to conduct training at the same time we were building a camp from scratch on a piece of that property forever after known to us tankers as "Jacque's Farm." Rip led the tank school through all its stages of evolution, retraining the faculty and students on each new vehicle and new tactical concept emerging from the war. He primarily accomplished this by letting us captains take care of things, and he had several good ones, including Lou Metzger, who later commanded the first armored amphibian battalion and retired as a lieutenant general. Rip was promoted to lieutenant colonel in June, 1943, and later com-

Here I am touring the Jacque's Farm tank training area in a jeep in the summer of 1943. Lew Griffin is driving and a LIFE magazine photographer is in the back.

manded the last battalion formed at the tank school, the 5th Tank Battalion, and led it on Iwo Jima. He subsequently became the first active-duty general to come from the ranks of World War II tank unit commanders.

Rip had only a few meetings with us staff officers. He left the day-to-day running of the camp to Capt. Olin Beall, his executive officer, a caricature of the Old Corps. At that time, Beall had no real knowledge of tanks. He had been left behind because of his age by the 2d Tank Battalion, which had first camped at Jacque's Farm before going overseas. So he had sort of come with the place. He later went to the army's tank school at Fort Knox and continued to serve at Jacque's Farm late in the war. During the first part of the Korean War, Beall commanded the 1st Motor Transport Battalion and performed heroically in the Chosin Reservoir campaign.

An old-time marine who enlisted at the age of seventeen, Beall loved putting second lieutenants in their place. I was sitting in his office once having coffee with him, talking about the training day, and somebody knocked on his door. In marched 2d Lt. Robert Ball, reporting for training duty. Bob Ball was a large man and sported a banged up nose—something that was appropriate for an All-American tackle from Notre Dame, which he had left just a few months earlier. Beall left him at attention and turned to me. "You know, Captain Neiman," he said. "I was just talking to the Training Command yesterday, and I told them I needed another officer student. I told them to send me the biggest, the ugliest, the dumbest lieutenant they had, and I'll be goddamned if they didn't do it!" He turned back toward Ball and roared, "See the sergeant major!"

Come the next morning, the same thing happened. This time it was 2d Lt. Robert Reed reporting in. Beall walked over to Reed, who stood rigidly at attention, and pulled his pistol, which he always carried, out of his holster. He pushed the muzzle against Reed's stomach and said, "Reed, I'd just as soon shoot you as look at you! See the sergeant major!" Reed retorted, "You say it and I'll carry it out, sir," and marched out. Reed actually had a short fuse, but he managed to keep his head. Later on, Reed and I became the best of friends.

Ed Bollard was an interesting, pugnacious new lieutenant, a real wise guy who proved to be a good man to have on your side in a fight. I almost took him for my company, but did not. Beall was showing three of these new officers around Jacque's Farm one day. Walking down the path, he saw yet another opportunity to put down the youngsters. Since his days as a marine gunner, Beall had taken to wearing his pistol strapped low on his thigh to facilitate a quick draw. He added to this his habit of thrusting his pistol into a new second lieutenant's belly at the slightest provocation. Spying a pop bottle about thirty feet away, he drew his pistol and fired so quickly that he could not even aim. He missed the bottle, but kicked up the dirt next to it, which made the bottle move. He blew on the barrel, pretty impressed with himself, holstered the pistol, and looked at the lieutenants. "Anybody think they can do any better?" He asked. This wise guy Bollard said, "Well, my arm is in a sling, but I'd like to try it left-handed." Beall, who did not know that Bollard was a natural southpaw, handed him the pistol. Bollard aimed it and cracked the bottle wide open. Beall angrily grabbed the pistol back and stomped off, leaving them there. I was watching this from the side and had quite a chuckle. Beall was just a character, and he remained totally unrepentant as long as I knew him. I heard later that a stalwart lieutenant who became one of Lou Metzger's company commanders cured him of his pistol-pulling antics.

We had our hands full at the tank school because we received a new tank model almost every month. There were no tactics manuals, just technical manuals and nomenclature lists for the vehicles. I never saw any tactical training films at Jacque's Farm, just a few that covered maintenance. We drew up our own training plans and organized each lesson as we saw fit, emphasizing practical application whenever possible. We had the help of several factory representatives, primarily for teaching the maintenance men, and they were some great guys. They lived with us and provided a lot of local knowledge for us whenever we needed them. We had one man from General Motors who taught us the hydromatic transmission. I was on the staff there for only six months, before I received orders to form my own tank company.

I personally never attended any tank school courses. When I formed my tank company at nearby Camp Pendleton, I immediately sent several officers and NCOs to the army armor course at Fort Knox, and the maintenance officer to General Motors for their engine and transmission course. That left only me and one lieutenant with which to organize the company. Fortunately, we had a lot of experience among the staff and factory reps at the tank school, and we managed to turn out a lot of able tankers. For instance, the muster rolls show that in June, 1943, we had forty-six second lieutenants and 1,086 enlisted men, although some of these served on the staff.

One of the drills I created at the school involved providing close protection for the tanks. Remembering what Leo Case had told me on Guadalcanal about the problem of the Japanese sneaking up and assaulting tanks in night positions, I devised a field exercise to improve everybody's skills. Taking both officers and men to the field, I wanted to emphasize the method of defending tanks in a bivouac. I split the class and set them to work on each mission, defender and aggressor, so that they would learn it from both sides. During the day, I sent a tank platoon to the field several miles away with orders to set up their bivouac site. The second lieutenant in command would position the tanks and organize his men to protect against infiltrators when it got dark. The other group of students, led by the Lieutenant Reed I had met in Beall's office, was then ordered to plan an attack on the platoon. I issued them bags of flour to simulate blowing up the tanks with satchel

This is me with signal flags in a posed publicity shot.

charges, and gave Reed two compass headings and said there was a tank platoon located between them about two miles distant. Their mission was to detect the position with scouts and attack the platoon. The lieutenant in charge of the defense proved to be pretty sharp. He moved a few guys to another hill and had them build a fire to decoy the enemy. Reed saw the flames, and decided to rush the position. They approached in single file, moving rapidly in the dark to a hill next to the one with the fire. In doing so, they stumbled right into the tank platoon's position. As they bunched up to plan their final move, the tanks turned on their headlights and simulated wiping them out. I was really tough on the attackers in my critique, especially Reed. In seeking to emphasize the errors they had made and I ended up chewing Reed out in front of all the others. That is a violation of good leadership, but they were all students and I wanted to press the points home. Reed later told me that he thought I was an SOB and said he would have liked to kill me on the spot. That was my second contact with him, but things soon improved. I was overawed to learn that the Marine Corps Tank School continued to use the flour-bag close assault drill I devised until 1970 to teach close protection to its students. The school was closed in 1973, after which all marine tankers were sent to the army's tank school at Fort Knox.

■ ■ ■

We had all kinds of tanks at Jacque's Farm: all of the M3 variants with both gas and diesel engines, the new M5A1s with their twin Cadillacs and hydromatic transmissions, and a few of the new M4 medium tanks. All of these tanks, and even the Marmon-Herringtons, were in use with various units across the Pacific. This happened because most of the defense battalions were assigned tank platoons after Wake Island fell, and the three tank battalions had a variety of light tank models. We formed the first medium tank battalion as a corps-level reinforcing unit in early 1943. The last of those infernal Marmon-Herringtons remained in use until 1943 with a couple of separate tank companies formed in mid-1942.

The CO of the 1st Corps Tank Battalion had some kind of political pull. His father was a senior staff officer on the FMF staff, I think, and he got command of the battalion as a major, after we put him through the tank course at Jacque's Farm. I think he may have been the only major to be assigned as a student there. At any rate, Bennet Powers asked me to be his executive officer, but I wanted no part of that. Somehow he managed to obtain Maj. Arthur J. Stuart as his exec right after "Jeb" finished the Fort Knox course as a distinguished graduate. The corps tank battalion was designed to land medium tanks from Landing Ships, Tank (LSTs), as reinforcements after the assault waves secured the beach. The battalion never operated together, although a couple of its companies deployed for landings, including 1st Lt. Ed Bale's C Company, which made a key contribution at Tarawa. The battalion was disbanded after that, and we all received new medium tanks in the divisional battalions. Powers never worked with tanks again, and Jeb Stuart survived his service with that troubled unit to become one of the guiding lights in the Marine Corps tank arm. I wanted only one of the lieutenants assigned to Powers's battalion for my company, and I eventually got him after it disbanded.

I spent a lot of time making lists of men and officers I thought I could use in my own tank company, where I would need five officers and almost two hundred men. One of the guys I had in mind was Bob Reed. Despite seeing him take some hard knocks early on, it turned out that Reed was a natural leader. He had attended Slippery Rock State Teachers' College at a time when everybody there majored in physical education, and he had apparently been a very good football player. Although short and stocky in stature, he was the quarterback in their second undefeated season in the fall of 1939. They played a New Year's Day game in Boston against undefeated Boston University and won.

Bob graduated in the spring of 1940 and volunteered for aviation cadet training in the Army Air Corps. One thing he struggled with constantly was his quick-fused temper. While on a training flight with an instructor, he baled out of the plane during a barrel roll to get back at the instructor and that finished his brief flying career. However, the flight school was one of those civilian contract schools doing feeder basic flight training for the services, and the director told Reed the only thing he thought anyone as crazy as he was ought to do was join the marines. So Bob went right over and did just that, enlisting in the Marine Corps as a private. He made corporal about a year later, and was assigned to Gen. Joseph W. Ernshaw's office in Headquarters, Marine Corps (HQMC). The general served on some promotion boards and Reed brought him his lunch each day. I guess Reed impressed him, and we know now that Bob had a photographic memory. Anyway, Ernshaw asked him if he was a college graduate and then asked him if he wanted to go to Officer Candidate School (OCS). When Reed said yes, Ernshaw asked him to recite the General Orders. Reed rattled the ten orders off without hesitation. According to Bob, Ernshaw picked up the phone and said, "Colonel [LePage] Cronmiller please." There was a pause and then he said, "When is the next class for Quantico, please?" After another pause he said, "Put Corporal Reed on that list." Reed attended OCS, and then came to Camp Elliott, where they assigned him to Jacque's Farm.

Bob was on the list of officers I wanted for my company, and being the senior of the second lieutenants, he ended up taking the 1st Platoon. When Steve Horton took A Company, Reed became my executive officer, and after Iwo he took over the company as a newly minted captain. My replacement for Reed had also been on my original list. I felt good about Reed. He proved to be a very hardworking conscientious officer with his platoon. Our relationship was later forged in fire. We each risked our own lives to save the other, worked together in harrowing combat, and we worked to make our company the best in the Marine Corps. As such, we developed complete faith and trust, and learned so much about each other's strengths and weaknesses that we remained together after the war. We made a great team and we figured out early on that Reed was an ideal detail and "inside" man, whereas I was better at coming up with ideas and outside work, the so-called front man. This remained as true in peacetime as it was in war.

Another of the best picks I made from the tank school was Gearl M. "G. M." English, a platoon sergeant who had gone to Iceland in mid-1941 with the first USMC tanks sent overseas, a dozen M2A4s from A Company, 2d Tank Battalion. He was by far the best driving instructor I had, and he was perhaps the most experienced of anyone at the school—with the exception of Rip Collins, who had joined the 1st Tank Company with its Marmon-Herringtons back in 1939. English proved to be such an able trainer and leader that I begged Rip to get him a field commission so I could make him a platoon commander. This he managed to do, and I was able to get G. M. for my company. In August, 1950, G. M. distinguished himself leading the first Marine Corps tank company into Korea as a captain.

Picking good NCOs and tank crewmen for the company posed little problem for me because I had the school staff at my disposal as screeners. I even had the luxury of picking a crewman who had been a professional photographer in civilian life. I asked Cpl. John C. Schutt if he would mind being the company photographer as an additional duty. I told him I thought it would be good for the company's morale if we had formal and candid pictures of everything we did, and Schutt agreed immediately. One of our senior NCOs obtained some still and motion picture cameras from chief petty officers at the San Diego navy base. The wrinkle they used was to designate Schutt as an official U.S. Navy photographer, and then sign over all the necessary equipment and film. In similar fashion, I took the services of Charles "Chilly" Newman, an administrative clerk then working for Olin Beall, to make sure that I had some talent in my company office.

My Dad came out to visit me while I was working at Jacque's Farm. I had not seen him since we our farewell in 1942 before I flew to San Francisco and went to the South Pacific. Dad stayed with me for a two- or three-day weekend. As he prepared to leave, he said: "Before I go I want a serious word with you about finances. How much are you saving out of your captain's pay? That's a lot of money."

"Are you nuts?" I replied a bit boisterously. "I'm not saving any of it. What for? I'll be going to war. I don't know if I'll survive. I'm going to have my fun while I can."

A captain could have a lot of fun in Southern California then, and I spent my pay as fast I was making it. Dad convinced me to the contrary by arguing that there was a good chance that I *would* make it, and it would be a nice thing to have a nest egg when I returned. I had to agree that it was stupid to piss it away, and I vowed to save some of it. Bob Reed and I agreed to each take out an allotment to create nest eggs if we had the luck to survive. These funds later became the seed money for the Neiman-Reed Lumber Company. Dad also wanted me to sell my Plymouth to a doctor, but I refused. I thus had use of the car after the war and later sold it in 1948 for twice what I had paid.

■   ■   ■

In December, 1943, Reed and I knew we were shipping out soon. Bob wanted to buy an engagement ring for a girl who lived on Poinsettia Place in Hollywood. She wanted to get married right away, but he thought it was foolish to do so with us on the verge of going off to war. In the end, he relented—at least to the point of getting her a ring. We each drew an advance on our pay and pooled our funds for the ring. However, the question remained: where should we go to buy it? San Diego was full of sharp sales characters. The safest bet seemed to be the Camp Pendleton Post Exchange, as regulations limited the markup to only 10 percent. We wound up buying a ring there for several hundred dollars using our joint money.

At first Reed's girl wrote every day. When we got to Maui after the Roi-Namur assault, over a month later, he had a huge pile of letters. Then, on Saipan, after a week or more of combat, a single letter finally came through. An infantry battalion commander, fearing a counterattack, had asked that our tanks stay forward in order to cover the road leading into our lines from the Japanese side. From this position, we saw a Mars flying boat land in the lagoon and we knew that mail would soon be coming up. Morale immediately began to improve. At dusk, my faithful "gofer," Pvt. Wayland Ashcraft, came up the hill with a mail sack, one letter already in hand. He told me he had the company mail, and I said, "Not tonight, we can't have men showing lights to read it, take it back to the rear." He replied, "But I have one here from Poinsettia Place." Before I could say anything, Reed grabbed the letter from him and dove under his tank with his poncho and flashlight.

He was not there very long before he stuck his face out from between the bogie wheels. It was as white as the paper. "Here, read this," he said. My first reaction was, "Now that's a real buddy for you, he's sharing his mail." So I got under the poncho and read the first lines of a "Dear John" letter. So much for our dead horse. I bugged Bob later to get the ring back, which he did. A few years after the war, when we were in Los Angeles and short of money, he decided to cash it in. We had spent $600 on it in 1943, so he asked a jeweler for an appraisal. After looking it over the guy told him it was a fake and offered $25 for it. A girlfriend suggested that we take it to a trusted jeweler friend of her family. This man said, "You should have taken the $25!" Our first thought was that the gal had taken it and replaced it with glass, but later we read that a marine captain, the officer in charge of the exchange at Pendleton, had just been sentenced to Portsmouth Naval Prison for defrauding customers and taking bribes for selling shoddy merchandise. We figured we must have bought glass in the first place. Our early experiences with finances did not bode well for the future.

One of the old Quantico lieutenants from 1941 showed up about this time and provided me with some unique experiences. I met Jack Conger, one of the Corps's early aces, while I was in the 1st Scout Company. Now, in 1943, the air wing had the idea of sending new pilots of fighters and dive-bombers down from El Toro Marine Corps Air Station to Camp Pendleton to observe ground training and the kinds of units they would support in combat. Jack was in charge of such a detail, and it was a lot of fun for the pilots. We took them in our tanks to the Windmill Canyon driving area (now a golf course) at Camp Pendleton. It measured three-fourths of a mile across the mouth and narrowed to less than half that at its end two or three miles farther up. We enjoyed scaring the hell out of the pilots, taking one in the bow gunner's seat and the other in the loader's hatch of an M5 and giving them a harrowing ride up one side of the canyon and across to the other. Just looking at it, nobody would think that a tank could handle the grade while crossing the ditch containing the dry riverbed. However, we had mastered it after weeks of practice and knew all the spots where you could cross and climb.

Conger thought it was great, but said he wanted a ride, too. I took him out in my tank, alone, and gave him a wild ride. I was a fool for doing it, though. When it was over, Jack told me that he had a new fighter, an F4U Corsair, and he could take out the radio and squeeze me in for a ride. So, he wanted to know, how about it? Well, I was cornered. With no way to decline gracefully, I agreed. The day came when Jack flew down to pick me up. We went up and he flew over Windmill Canyon where we could watch the tanks. Suddenly he shouted, "Here we go!" and the next thing I knew, we were diving straight down at the dry riverbed. At the last second he pulled out and we shot up the narrow canyon wall, skimming the ground. One of his wings clipped the antenna off G. M. English's tank, we were so low. I remember thinking, this guy is crazy, as we hurtled past the power lines on one side of the canyon and zoomed up to six thousand feet with me hanging on for dear life. Jack asked me if I had had enough, and I could not say anything. He took that for a "no" and we reversed direction and did it all again. Then we landed and called it tit for tat. That was the aviation indoctrination and exchange program for 1943!

While I was at Jacque's Farm I learned of the death of Capt. Bruce Mattson, the commander of the 2d Separate Tank Company on Uvea Island, north of Samoa. This was a strange company set up to take the last of the Marmon-Herrington tanks ordered by the Marine Corps, including five of the latest ones, which had finally been fitted with turrets. I was told that he had been killed in an accident and assumed it was a plane crash or something like that. Not until long after the war was over did I learn that Bruce had committed suicide. He had been despondent over the death of one of his troops on a rifle range where he had prematurely given the okay to open fire. It was Bruce who had given me my first tank lesson, ending in the last ride of Marie in the 1st Scout Company. He was a fine man, and I was sorry to see him meet such an end. However, we were going to lose many more like him during the next two years.

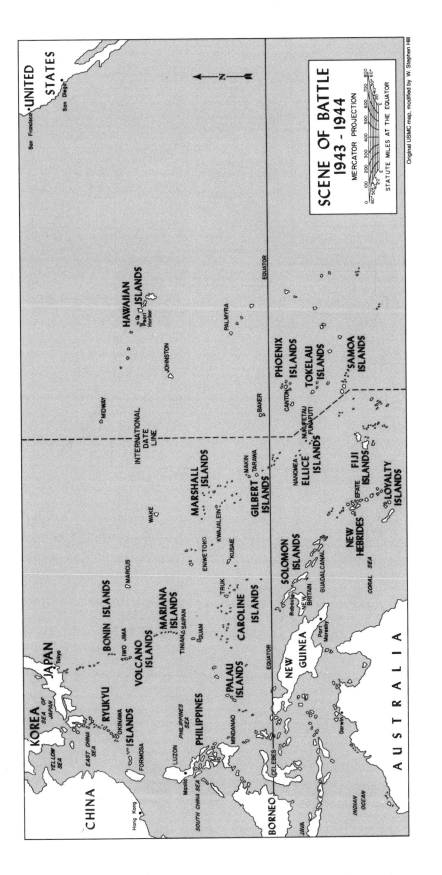

SCENE OF BATTLE
1943 - 1944

MERCATOR PROJECTION

STATUTE MILES AT THE EQUATOR

0 100 200 300 400 500 600 700 800

Original USMC map, modified by W. Stephen Hill

CHAPTER 6

Gearing Up
for the Central Pacific

Roi-Namur

The 4th Tank Battalion was formed on May 12, 1943, but only on paper. The tank companies remained separate because the 4th Marine Division's infantry regiments were scattered, too. We even had a scout company, Company D, with each of its platoons attached to the regiments, but it later went to the division. The 23d and 24th Marines organized and did their initial training at New River. Only the 25th Marines stood up at Camp Pendleton.

The regiments remained apart for at least six months before the division was finally united at Camp Pendleton in September, 1943. In July, however, the tank companies had been gathered together under the command of Maj. Richard K. Schmidt at Camp Pendleton, and our own training improved. Dick was the son of Maj. Gen. Harry Schmidt, the division commander. That would prove both an advantage and disadvantage to us, in the following months. I liked Dick a lot, but he did not show me much knowledge as a tanker, even though he had been a platoon leader in Robert L. "Bob" Denig Jr.'s B Company, 2d Tank Battalion, the first tank unit sent to Samoa in 1942. Of course, there was little to learn there except maintenance in the tropics and driving on roads. We were the only battalion in the Marine Corps to receive a complete issue of the new M5A1 light tanks. It was a lot better than the M3, with more room, a little more armor, and an escape hatch placed in the tank's belly under the assistant driver's position. It still had only the 37-mm popgun, but what a power plant! Its twin Cadillac V-8 engines drove the only automatic transmission we ever saw in tanks. It was a real joy to drive. The decision to field the M4 Sherman as the new standard issue vehicle interrupted the wholesale procurement of M5A1 light tanks, though, and only the 4th Tank Battalion received a complete M5 issue. Proper deepwater fording kits and waterproofing materials ensured the safe and rapid landing of all new tanks, and we now could ford seven feet of water.

We officially formed A Company, 4th Tank Battalion, at Jacque's Farm on June 8, and moved right away to a barracks area at Camp Pendleton. In November, we traded in our light tanks for new M4 medium tanks. I think Dick Schmidt thought the medium tank company in the new light-medium tank battalion organization was to be the third one, so he changed our designation to C Company. Other than these administrative details, Dick left us company commanders to our own devices, which was fine by me, as I had a perfect picture of what I wanted to accomplish. Looking back, I think we made a big mistake in not coordinating the efforts of all the companies and agreeing on set procedures and so forth. But with a battalion commander who thought differently, we were left to our own devices.

You may recall that Rip Collins had told me I could handpick personnel for my company, and that I had even resorted to assigning some men to the Jacque's Farm staff in order to keep them around for the company's formation. I already had English and Reed earmarked, but I was still looking for another platoon leader when I first saw Hank Bellmon. I was in my jeep, watching about fifteen tanks conducting driving practice. One of the tanks came up fast, spun to a halt, and threw a track. It was an M5. The guy in the turret stayed with his driver to talk him forward and backward while two crewmen dismounted and got the track back on in no time at all. As they were climbing back in, I walked over and talked to the commander, a big guy, and asked his name. "Second Lieutenant Henry Bellmon, sir," he replied. I asked when he had reported to tank school. "A week ago, sir," he said. When I asked how he learned to fix a thrown track so fast, he said, "Sir, I've been around farm equipment all my life except for college, and I've been doing it since I was six years old."

The original officers of C Company, 4th Tank Battalion, 1943.
BACK ROW, FROM LEFT: me; 2d Lt. G. M. English, who as a captain
commanded the marine tank company sent to the Pusan
perimeter in 1950; and 2d Lt. Henry Bellmon, who later
served two terms as governor and as a senator from
Oklahoma. FRONT ROW, FROM LEFT: 2d Lt. Bob Reed;
2d Lt. Gil Bradley, maintenance officer; and 1st Lt.
Steve Horton, who later commanded A Company.

I immediately determined that this guy would make a good platoon leader. He did. I later recommended him for a Silver Star on Iwo. He had gone to Oklahoma State and then joined the Marine Corps after Pearl Harbor. He remained in the Marine Corps Reserve after the war and went back to the farm. A truly conservative man, he was deeply religious, and never swore nor drank nor smoked nor went out with girls who did. After each assault landing, he sent soil samples back to his agronomy professor at Oklahoma State. When he returned from the war, a group of Young Republicans looking for a candidate to run for governor decided Henry was their man. Oklahoma was close to 100 percent Democratic back then, but they mounted one hell of a campaign and he became the state's first Republican governor. He became so popular that the legislature amended the state law to allow him to serve a second term. He refused to run, though, and went back to the farm. Then Sen. Andrew Kerr retired and Henry again became the Republican choice. He won, and wound up serving two terms in the U.S. Senate. Years later, he would serve two more terms as governor. We were very close, but Henry later published a book in which he characterized me as a real playboy. Bellmon was a fine Marine, the kind of fellow we need in politics but never seem to have in sufficient quantities. When I left the battalion later, Henry wrote his brother, a gunnery sergeant in the 6th Tank Battalion on Okinawa, where I was headed. This guy, who was even bigger than Henry, came to visit me during the battle while I was executive officer of the 1st Tank Battalion.

Some time late on that first day of our existence as A Company, I formed up the men and talked to them for the first time. It was really a pep talk, and what I remember best about it is that I let everybody know they had been handpicked. I congratulated them on this, and told them we were the best of the best, and then said that we would train very hard and become the best tank company in the Marine Corps. Everybody cheered. I felt very proud of my speech. Later that day, my executive officer, 1st Lt. Steve Horton, and two of my platoon commanders, Reed and English, and several of the NCOs left for a four-week course at the U.S. Army Armor School at Fort Knox. My maintenance officer, 2d Lt. Gilbert Bradley, and several mechanics went to a month-long course at the factory making the M5A1, which had the hydromatic transmission. The only other officer present for duty was Hank Bellmon, with whom I bunked in a new barracks and thus came to know a lot better.

■   ■   ■

By the time the men returned from their schools, the entire 4th Tank Battalion had been formed and the tanks moved from the "civilized" part of Camp Pendleton to a training area at Aliso Canyon a few miles north of the main base. We were out on our own, living in tents, with no paved roads, no communications wire strung across the trails, and we could make as much noise and raise as much dust as we wanted. It gave us a chance to become a well-trained tank company, doing the necessary driving, shooting, and maintenance. We now needed to train with the infantry in order to become part of the division team. We knew we had to orient the division to tanks and the need to train with tanks and infantry together. It was up to us tankers to do the teaching. The infantry officers at company and battalion level were interested and willing, but the regimental commanders proved to be harder cases for us to convince.

We used a lot of training areas at Camp Pendleton for training the company. Most of our training consisted of tank crew drills and unit battle drills like the ones I had organized at Jacque's Farm. The main thing was to get each platoon used to working as a team and then maneuvering together as a company.

We spent six months at Pendleton, three of them absolutely alone without the battalion or the infantry regiments. The second three months we trained with division units. The company usually worked with the 23d Marines, and it was during this training that we developed the tank-infantry tactics that served us so well later in the Central Pacific. However, before we trained with the infantry, we did two types of crew drills that interested me. We taught both driving and gunnery at the tank school, but learning how to shoot and move at the same time was very important.

One drill for shooting and maneuvering became a kind of competition. We assigned a color to each tank and gave the crew a can of enamel paint bought at a local paint store. The crews then dipped the tips of the .30-caliber bullets in their coaxial machine-gun ammo belts into the paint and so marked their ammo. One platoon would then attack the other in a tactical problem. As they maneuvered over the rolling hills, there would be a surprise encounter with the "enemy." We would then have a tank versus tank "fight" in which the gunners fired their coax machine gun one round at a time as if it were the main gun.[1] After it was over, we debriefed the unit on its maneuver and counted the colored scratches left by the bullets. The platoon that scored the most hits won.

We got away with this because we had learned that the company would be receiving new medium tanks and that we would be turning in our M5A1s. It did not matter how badly scarred their hulls and turrets were from these training bullets. The guys had a hell of a lot of fun with this drill. They learned how to react quickly and shoot accurately (less so while moving, although we did use the vertical gyrostabilizer) and enjoyed it while they were doing it.

The other drill was aimed at improving rapid-reaction driving skills. We painted the bow of each tank with a different color then sent two platoons out to maneuver against each other, allowing the drivers to lightly "tag" opposing vehicles if possible. This taught each driver and tank commander a lot about rapid maneuvering, handling the levers and pedals to brake and steer and reverse and either strike or avoid another tank's moves. With the M5 tank, they did not have to shift except for changing from forward to reverse, but the rest was complicated. At the end, we tallied the colored marks on the various tanks in order to determine the winner. As with the shooting drill, we had a lot of fun playing "tank tag" and developed some really crucial skills.

The most fun, though, came after the final divisional maneuver, which involved boarding the USS *Gunston Hall* (LSD-5) for practice landings and then returning to San Diego. As we were unloading, some sailors noticed how badly marked up our tanks were. Since we had just returned from an unknown place in the broad Pacific Ocean, a rumor quickly spread around the piers that we were an outfit just back from combat. They did not know that we had only been to San Clemente Island for a landing exercise. Of course, our guys encouraged this speculation and soon the swabbies were swarming all over our tanks and our guys were selling helmets, tank parts, and anything else they could strip off the vehicles as war trophies. They really made some money that day!

In combat, we operated the tanks buttoned up most of time. That meant all hatches were shut and the crew looked out through periscopes and gun sights. We communicated with the outside world with our radios, but they did not always work. Fortunately, we had pushbutton channel selection on the army-issue SCR radios. I had a channel for each platoon leader, and one for a company-wide net that all tanks monitored. Then I had a channel for my liaison officer, usually the company exec, with the higher headquarters. The best answer to any problem was training. We trained to deal with any kind of action we thought we might encounter. It became second nature for the platoon leaders and NCOs to know what to do in a specific situation. However, before we started out, I made sure everybody knew what we were doing, so they could then fight their own tank and contribute toward the unit mission. If I spotted something first, I would call it out and assign a platoon or individual tanks to take the target out. The drills were thus worked out, and training proved the essence of it all.

Tank training is twofold. First there is technical training on how to operate vehicles, break track, fire weapons, and so forth. Then there is tactical training. This covers how we employ tanks, what formations we use, what kind of ammo is best for a variety of different targets, rate of fire, and so forth. If we came under antitank fire, there were three things we would try to do. First, of course, we would try to knock out the antitank gun with our own fire. At the same time, we would fire smoke (white phosphorous) projectiles to obscure the enemy's vision. We also worked at presenting a less vulnerable target by moving into hull defilade and turning to face the enemy with our thick frontal armor. Then we worked hard at keeping track of our own infantry so we would not fire on them and also so they would be nearby in case the enemy infantry launched a close assault.

One of our most trusted and best techniques was firing at each other with machine guns when the enemy infantry tried to pile on. We had planned on this early, because I knew that at Guadalcanal the biggest problem the tanks faced was the Japanese infantry. On the second morning of the landing on Namur, I was in my command post monitoring a platoon that was out with the infantry. Suddenly, Mike Giba, one of the tank commanders, shouted excitedly over the platoon net, "This guy is looking at me, right down my periscope!" Apparently the Japanese had swarmed all over his tank, and he was announcing it to the world. Then came the calming voice of Hank Bellmon, his platoon leader, saying very coolly and calmly, "Don't worry Mike, we're shooting them as fast as they get on there, just stay where you are 'cause it's giving us good targets." And that's the way it worked. The other tanks were firing and wiping the enemy off.

You quickly got used to looking at the world through periscopes. By the time we assaulted Iwo, the new tanks had vision rings around the commander's cupola, which helped a lot. Except for Iwo, we brought our surviving tanks back each time and turned them in for a new set before the next operation began. For somebody new, being buttoned up in a tank is a weird experience. Except for your periscopes, you cannot see a goddamn thing and for some people it is a real fright—and I do not mean that derogatorily. It is just that some people's system cannot take it. We discovered that about 10 percent of the men in each class at the tank school would get claustrophobia when buttoned up. G. M. English and I figured this out at Jacque's Farm. English said, "You know, Captain, we're wasting a lot of time trying to train these guys." So we decided to give every man a ride in a buttoned-up tank on the first day of training. Just as we had calculated, one in ten would throw up. We would send these guys back to the replacement camp at Camp Elliott the next day, instead of wasting our time trying to make tankers out of them. The people who remained felt more or less at home. Regardless of how skilled we became, though, the vision was very poor in the older M3 light tanks, and we felt fortunate that we never had to fight in them.

The Landing Ship, Dock (LSD; a transport with a dry-dock installed aft to float out and recover landing craft), had a lot of different people on board: the ship's crew, marines, and an amphibious group consisting of an ensign and crews for the eighteen landing craft, mechanized (LCM), that carried us in our tanks to the shore. The ensign in charge of the landing craft coxswains was a jerk. He insisted that his LCM would take me, since I was the company commander. That was okay by me, as the coxswain was doing the maneuvering and this guy just rode along. When we hit the beach during the first practice landing, the damn ramp would not go down. We finally had to get two or three other crewmen together, jimmy the ramp, and then lower it so I could get off. I told the ensign that he had to get that ramp fixed for the next maneuver, or I would go through it. The same thing happened the next time. We then sailed for Kwajalein, and I promised the guy that if it happened during the operation, I was not going to wait. I would go right through it. He assured me that it would work. Nevertheless, when we hit the reef at Roi, the ramp would not go down. I told the driver to go through it. We went up to it, forced our way through it, and left that LCM without a ramp. The captain of the *Gunston Hall* later told me that the crew managed to get towed back to the ship. He then loaned them a few ship fitters and they managed to repair the broken ramp. My driver, Thomas J. Taylor, took great delight in going through that thing.

I knew that a lot of guys on Guadalcanal went without dental care for a long time, and that many of them had problems. I did not want that to happen to me, so I went to the dental dispensary at the Camp Pendleton naval hospital. I had not been to the dentist for a long time, and I apparently needed a few fillings. The dentist said I was okay now, however. A week or so later, while on liberty in Los Angeles on a Sunday morning, I was eating some scrambled eggs and a tooth broke off. I was madder than hell, having just been to the dentist. With fire in my eyes, I went looking for the dentist and told him off. "I knew that tooth was bad," he replied, "but I thought I could save it with a filling. I should not have done that." We finally agreed that he should pull the remainder of the tooth and construct a bridge. After he pulled the tooth, he told me that we would have to wait three weeks for the hole to heal. Fortunately, I was still there after three weeks. But when I reported back he said that I would have to go to the orthodontic section. I was really getting mad at this point. The navy captain in charge of that section laughed at me. "Do you really think the Navy is going to worry about replacing just one tooth when many Marines are missing a dozen or more?" he asked. "We don't have enough time to do all of them, so we certainly can't take the time to do just one tooth. The only time we'll put in a tooth if you're missing one is if you lose it in combat." I was madder than hell. We argued, but he won. Some months later, when we reached our new base camp at Maui, I wrote a phony story saying that I had lost the tooth during the battle of Roi, when I hit my head inside the tank. They finally replaced the tooth while I was on Maui, and they did a good job, too, even though they had to use foot-powered equipment. I wore that bridge for about twenty years, before I finally had it replaced. That was my one and only experience with navy dentistry.

■   ■   ■

Changing to the M4A2 medium tank was a real delight. We had a little experience with them at Jacque's Farm, but the company maintenance people had a lot to learn, so we sent the maintenance officer, Gil Bradley, and a half-dozen or so men to a short course at Fort Knox. We had some M4 medium tanks at Jacque's Farm for training, and they came in three varieties. The shapes of the hulls varied a bit, too. Some were rounded and some were sharp-cornered, but they generally looked about the same. The Chrysler engines in the first M4A4 we had at Jacque's Farm were an abomination. Chrysler, since it did not have an engine designed expressly for tanks, improvised with five automobile engines that came right off their line. These were joined together in a radial fashion. Thus, each "engine" had five water pumps, five carburetors, and so forth. What a nightmare they were. I do not think they ever went overseas. The General Motors engines in our own M4A2 were twin 225-

horsepower diesels, and the M4A3 had the single Ford GAA, which used gasoline but still proved to be a good engine. We liked the diesel the most because it would lug down and maintain its torque. In the end, however, we wound up taking the Ford-powered tanks to Iwo because they were all we could get from the army supply system. They preferred those gasoline-powered engines because they used the same kind of fuel as their trucks.

We did not call these tanks "Shermans" until after the war ended, and then usually only when speaking to civilians so as to make it clear what we had been using. During the war we simply called them "mediums" or " GMs" or "Fords" or "Chryslers" in order to distinguish the engine types.

A publicity shot of one of our new M4A2 medium tanks at the Training Command. The army did not employ this Sherman model in combat because it did not want diesel-powered vehicles overseas for supply reasons.

■ ■ ■

As 1943 came to an end, we thought that we were well prepared and equipped for the job ahead. We had trained with the 23d Marines, one of the division's three regiments of infantry (the others being the 24th and 25th Marines) at Pendleton, and had taught them a lot about how to take advantage of the tank. The division planned a demonstration of how tanks can go through a barrage of time-fused airbursts unharmed. The whole 4th Tank Battalion participated. As we moved through the impact area the shrapnel hitting our M5s sounded like rain on a tent. Everything went well, but we did have one casualty. Second Lieutenant Dick Pierson, one of A Company's platoon commanders, rode in a tank as the assistant driver.[2] One of the periscopes was missing and had only a sheet metal weather cap covering the hole it normally occupied. A shell fragment went right through it, wounding him severely in the thigh.

We worked hard with the infantry battalions, but we never convinced Col. Louis Jones, the 23d Marines regimental commander, of much. He was a very autocratic commander and I was just a captain. I made major before Saipan, however, and people started to listen to me. Even Colonel Jones became more appreciative of me. I later recommended that tank company commanders should be majors because they have to deal with battalion and regiment commanders all the time and those officers tend to pay more attention to majors than mere captains.

We loaded our tanks and boarded the USS *Gunston Hall* for the Kwajalein campaign, sailing on January 13, 1944. We were going into combat as a division, participating in the first amphibious attack undertaken directly from the United States. It also was the first assault on Japanese territory. All of the other islands we had taken thus far, including Tarawa, had been occupied by Japan after Pearl Harbor.

The first stop our convoy made after setting out from San Diego was Lahaina Roads, Maui, where the invasion convoy assembled. This was the first sight that any of us had ever had of Hawaii, all of us being from the Midwest or East Coast. When we pulled in, I asked the captain if I could take my officers ashore as long as I left one on board. He was amenable to that and arranged for a boat to put us ashore that afternoon. He advised us to be back on the pier at 5 P.M., as the convoy would sail that evening. We very happily agreed. We climbed up on the pier at 2 P.M. and immediately began looking for an island drink.

The village of Lahaina stood right at the end of the pier and there was an old hotel, the Pioneer Inn, one of only three hotels on the island. It

The skipper of the USS GUNSTON HALL, Comdr. Dale Collins, poses here with C Company's officers en route to our first assault at Roi-Namur. FROM LEFT IN REAR: Hank Bellmon, Bob Reed, Collins, and me. FROM LEFT IN FRONT: G. M. English and Gil Bradley, my maintenance officer. Steve Horton, my executive officer, was aboard another ship with the 23d Marines commander. He was doctrinally attached to the 23d Marines headquarters as the tank liaison officer.

was built in the nineteenth century and had no beach, but instead sat on a rocky shore. We noticed a sign at one corner of the hotel that read, "Old Whaler's Grog Shop." That sounded good to us, and we ambled on over to it. It appeared to be a typical South Pacific bar, with a screened-in porch on one side and a bar and tables on the other. The bartender, a big wide Hawaiian, said, "Come in, Marines!" He seemed pretty amazed to see us, as none were on Maui as yet. "My specialty is the 'harpoon'," he said. "Have you ever had one?" None of us had, so he made up a batch and we drank them right down. They went to our heads pretty quickly. After a few more, we were drunker than hell and never got out of the saloon to see anything of the island. As five o'clock rolled around, the coxswain of the launch swung alongside the pier and, finding no one waiting, was savvy enough to look for us at the bar. Between him and the bartender, they managed to get all five of us into the boat, although we had a hell of a time getting aboard the LSD. So went our first stop in the Hawaiian Islands.

■ ■ ■

At Kwajalein Atoll, the army was assigned the island of Kwajelein at the southern end of the lagoon and the 4th Marine Division drew the islands of Roi and Namur on the north side. The two small islands were connected by a causeway. The day before the assault landing, armored amphibian tractors (amtracs) landed some of the division's troops and artillery on five little islands located close by, to give us artillery support on D-Day, February 1. Ships plastered the islands as we circled around inside the lagoon, loaded in our eighteen LCMs. The armored amtracs and troop amtracs carrying the 23d Marines went in first and we touched down on Roi only minutes after them in shallow water not far from the shoreline. That island had the largest airfield in the

C Company's senior NCOs are shown here before the Roi-Namur landings. FROM LEFT IN REAR: Sgt. Joe Bruno, Gy.Sgt. Sam Johnston (I later made him the company gunnery sergeant), Sgt. Charles Ehrenfeld, S.Sgt. Norman S. Mayfield (chief cook), Sgt. Bill Downey (mess cook), Sgt. Russ Lippert, Sgt. Andrew Apone (maintenance), and 1st Sgt David W. Barrett (transferred after the battle). FROM LEFT IN FRONT: Sgt. Herman D. Lunsford (maintenance chief), Sgt. Earl G. Hopkins, Sgt. Raymond H. Shaw (maintenance), and Sgt. Gerald L. "Diddy-dot" De Moss (communications chief).

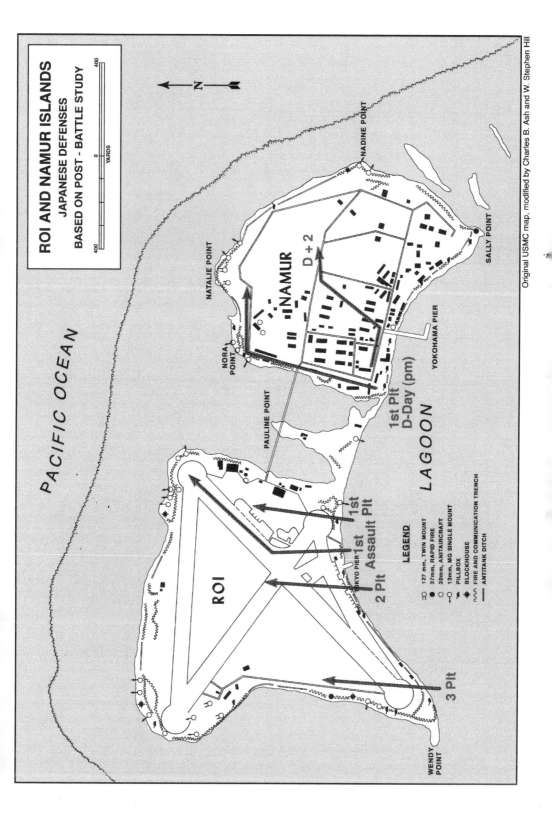

ROI AND NAMUR ISLANDS
JAPANESE DEFENSES
BASED ON POST - BATTLE STUDY

N

400 0 400
YARDS

PACIFIC OCEAN

NADINE POINT

SALLY POINT

NATALIE POINT

NAMUR

D + 2

NORA POINT

YOKOHAMA PIER

PAULINE POINT

1st Plt
D-Day (pm)

LAGOON

ROI

1st Plt

1st
Assault Plt

TOKYO PIER

2 Plt

3 Plt

WENDY POINT

LEGEND

- ♀ 127 mm, TWIN MOUNT
- ●○ 37mm, RAPID FIRE
- ○○ 20mm, ANITAIRCRAFT
- ✦ 13mm, MG SINGLE MOUNT
- ✚ PILLBOX
- ◆ BLOCKHOUSE
- ⌇⌇⌇ FIRE AND COMMUNICATION TRENCH
- ▬▬ ANTITANK DITCH

Original USMC map, modified by Charles B. Ash and W. Stephen Hill

Marshall Islands chain, with its three runways and taxi strips, and was almost devoid of any cover or obstacles. As we waded ashore in our tanks, we were filled with a growing tension. This was our first fight and we wondered what would happen to us. Suddenly I heard Hank Bellmon's voice on my command frequency. He had pressed the wrong button on his radio, intending to use his platoon net, and was unknowingly talking to the whole company. "Okay, men," he said. "There's only one more thing I want to tell you: This is it, I want you to keep a steady trigger finger and a tight asshole." And with that, the whole company burst into laughter. To hear Henry Bellmon of all people say that. We actually made our first assault landing with the whole company laughing. As we came ashore, I remember seeing a big antitank ditch just a few yards inland. I got out with my company gunny, Sam Johnston, and we found a section broken down by the naval gunfire bombardment. We then crossed the ditch, and formed up on line to support the attack across the island.

The runways crisscrossed the island, making it very flat and open. We headed up to the O-1 line, our first objective, using an open V for-

Hank Bellmon's 2d Platoon is shown here with him on the LEFT and his platoon sergeant, Russ Lippert, obscured by a helmet at the UPPER RIGHT. Also shown is the Maintenance Section, with 2d Lt. Gil Bradley. I made Lippert my company first sergeant after Roi-Namur. He was killed later on Iwo, right before my eyes.

mation. When we arrived there we found an infantry battalion setting in on the line, Lt. Col. Edward J. Dillon in command, and we were more or less supporting him at that point. He told us we would have to stop. About a thousand yards ahead on the north or seaward coast I could see six big blockhouses. I assumed that they were coast defense guns, but I had no idea whether they could turn on us. There was absolutely no cover on the island, and I could not see stopping and holding up forever, waiting for something to happen. I told Dillon I wanted to keep going and take the rest of the island. I could not see anything else that might hold us up except for those blockhouses, and I wanted to get over there and take them out before they made trouble for us. We argued a bit, and I finally asked for some infantry support.

"No," he said. "In fact, I'm ordering you to stay here."

I told him that was entirely against tank doctrine. "You don't stop and stay exposed in the open," I explained, "you keep moving."

"I'll have to tell Colonel Jones that you're not obeying his plan," he replied.

I already knew that the purpose of the O-1 line was to wait for additional naval gunfire to shift and cover the rest of the island. I also knew that it was just a matter of calling that fire off for the attack to resume, since we did not need it. So we went on, crossing the airfield, to the end of the island. There were no guns in the blockhouses. I later learned that one of my tank commanders, Joe Bruno, had blown up an intact Zero fighter, and they tried to give us hell for that. We bounced a few armor-piercing (AP) rounds off the blockhouses, but none of them penetrated. We received no return fire. We then spotted another anti-tank ditch across the north end of the island. Hundreds of Japanese troops were in there, hiding. We opened up on them, but could not depress our guns enough to bring effective fire on them. Then I lost Cpl. Joe Ramos. He was killed by a rifle shot when he looked out of his turret.

We continued firing at the enemy in the antitank ditch. I called back to our tank liaison officer at the regimental command post (CP), Steve Horton, and told him to tell the colonel that we had all the Japanese cornered, and to bring up the infantry so that we could finish them off. Steve's reply was that we had to leave them and come back, that we were holding up the naval gunfire that had been scheduled. I objected, saying that we did not need it. "Send the troops and the battle is over," I said.

At that point, Colonel Jones came on the net and read me the riot act. He told me in no uncertain terms to get my ass back to the regiment's lines. He assured me that when the battle ended I would be under house arrest, awaiting a general court-martial if we did not start moving immediately.

"We're on our way back, colonel," I replied. "But all these Japs are going to get away." Returning to the O-1 line and Lieutenant Colonel Dillon's battalion and seeing his sneering face, I told him the same thing. Anyway, the naval gunfire fired for its scheduled twenty minutes, after which we retraced our paths. Just as I had predicted, all the Japanese were gone. The island was declared secure. Shortly thereafter, we were told to get over to Namur and report to a Lieutenant Colonel Brunelli.

G. M. English, FAR RIGHT FRONT, and his 3d Platoon before the Roi-Namur landings. The platoon sergeant, Sgt. Joe Bruno, is at the FAR LEFT. SEATED SECOND FROM THE RIGHT IN THE FRONT ROW is Corporal Ramos, who was killed instantly by a sniper. He was the only man in my company killed on Roi-Namur. His assistant driver, Charles B. Ash, took over the tank and later became my driver. Ash is seen here in the RIGHT REAR, up against the metal locker, with his helmet tilted back. "C. B." was a wild one, but he stayed in the Marine Corps after the war and retired as master gunnery sergeant.

The 24th Marines did not assault Namur until later on D-Day morning because of delays in rounding up enough amtracs and landing craft. I found out later that the same amtracs had been used the day before to take the smaller islands for the artillery. Anyway, the 24th Marines had a much harder time securing Namur than we did taking Roi. That island had more varied terrain, including some thick foliage, and contained most of the defending garrison. Company B's light tanks began to land in the 24th Marines' zone an hour after we landed on Roi. Some of their M5A1s bogged down in sand and shell holes, but others succeeded in reaching the infantry on their O-1 line. Undergrowth and rubble concealed many of the surviving pillboxes, and the enemy's weapons slowed the advance and made it hard to mop up after they were bypassed. The Japanese attempted to swarm the light tanks with grenades and mines whenever possible, but in all but one case the infantry and tanks swept them away with fire. Captain Jim Denig, the company commander, led his headquarters section forward to replace a platoon he had pulled back for rearming. Attacking into the underbrush, Denig's tank veered out of line after striking a log and stopped, only to be attacked by a squad of Japanese. They threw a grenade into the turret through the signal port, which had inadvertently been left open, killing Denig and his gunner and setting the tank on fire.

I was shocked to learn of this. Jim had a premonition of his death a couple of days before embarking at Camp Pendleton. He had told me about his girlfriend, Mary Lou VanNess, whom he was planning on marrying. She was Bing Crosby's secretary at Paramount Pictures and was quite a gal, I later found out. All this weighed very heavily on his mind, because he gave me her address and said, "I just feel like I'm not going to make it and I want you to write and tell her what happened." Of course, I did just that. After the battle, when we got to Maui, I got a warm thank-you letter with a picture of a very pretty girl enclosed in response. We began corresponding, exchanging no more than a half-dozen letters over the next two years. I looked her up after the war and found that she was quite a nice girl. We went on a few dates, but it was more of a platonic thing, a lot of fun, but eventually she became serious with somebody else. She introduced me to Crosby, Bob Hope, and other celebrities. I did not find out until later that my eventual wife was working virtually side-by-side with her there at Paramount. I also did not know that Paramount would become one of my biggest corporate accounts. About thirty years later, Suzy and I attended a charity dinner

This M5A1 light tank, nicknamed "Hunter," is the one in which Jim Denig, the B Company commander, and almost all his crew died on Namur. The light tank could not cope with the Corps's missions in the Pacific War, so we converted to all medium tanks by the summer of 1944.

in the San Fernando Valley. After we finished eating, a young man in his twenties came up to me and asked if I was Bob Neiman. He was the former Mary Lou VanNess's son, and he said that I still looked like the picture of me his family had. It is indeed a small world.

I never saw Denig's tank, but I knew that the light tanks were not that effective in the brush. The planners assumed that the heaviest fighting would be on Roi, owing to the important airfield. They figured that Namur, which was a support base for Roi, would be easier. They thus assigned what they thought was the bigger job to the medium tanks, but it turned out to be just the opposite. General Schmidt, the division commander, ordered a reserve battalion and our mediums over to Namur to reinforce.

We crossed over our old landing beaches and a sandbar to Namur, where we found Lt. Col. Austin R. Brunelli and his battalion on the 24th Marines' left flank. He was waiting for me on a narrow beach running south to north along Namur's west coast. The jungle began right off the beach. "We can't get up the beach," Brunelli said. "There are pillboxes at the edge of the jungle, and we can't get through the fire. Can you clear it?" I said, "Sure, but could we have some infantry to go along, too?" He said he would have a rifle company accompany us.

The beach was too narrow for us to spread out, so we were forced to go single file in a column. I had one of our best NCOs, Earl G. "Hoppy" Hopkins, the 1st Platoon sergeant, follow me. I went first whenever we were in column. When on line, I would be in the center, preferably in a shallow V, so I could see everyone.

Every time we came to a pillbox—and there must have been seven or eight of them as we moved up the island—I would say to Hoppy over the radio: "There's a pillbox about seventy yards ahead. I'm going to poke this seventy-five right in the opening, so be damn sure you've got me covered." And he would say, "Roger, Congo [or whatever my code name was], we got you covered." I was concerned that as we got close to the edge of the jungle they might jump out on us, and I wanted to make sure Hoppy was covering us. He was, so we would go up and blast the hell out of each pillbox. Some were already empty because the troops had fired their weapons with no effect on us. We would put the muzzle of our 75-mm gun an arm's length from the aperture of the pillbox and fire a white phosphorus (WP) round into it, then send in a high-explosive (HE) round if they did not immediately run out. Platoon Sergeant Hopkins was a drunk and a brawler when on liberty, but when sober he was a very good NCO. He was the kind of guy you wanted on your side in a fight. A couple of my officers had suggested I leave him behind, but I wanted him with us in combat, and he did a good job. He was wounded on Saipan, and rejoined us after Iwo. He survived Okinawa, but his luck eventually ran out and he was killed in Korea. He was Reed's platoon sergeant, and Reed agreed with me about keeping him for the fighting. That judgment proved correct on D-Day at Kwajalein.

We went several hundred yards knocking off these pillboxes, and then the island curved east a short ways and we found ourselves at the north end of the island. Suddenly we were looking into a pair of 5-inch naval guns that the Japanese had emplaced, pointing right at us. This is it! I thought. We're done for! But the guns did not fire. I figured they must have been knocked out by air or artillery strikes or had a mechanical problem or run out of ammo. Then I spotted Japanese troops firing

machine guns down into marines on the jungle floor from secure spots
atop the gun barrels, about fifteen feet above the surrounding ground.
We maneuvered four or five tanks on line in the large open area in front
of the guns and shot these new "fish in a barrel" with our coax machine
guns. After they were all taken care of, our infantry caught up with us
and rooted out the survivors. By then it was beginning to get dark, so I
huddled up with the rifle company commander. We had lost contact
with the rest of the battalion in the heavy jungle while moving up on
the flank, and decided we had gone as far as we wanted to and that we
should withdraw back to Brunelli's position.

We were low on ammo and sent a working party back to Roi to look
for more 75-mm rounds, but all they could find were some pallets of
practice ammo. In all my time in the Marine Corps I had never seen any
practice ammunition, but that was what had been landed there on Roi.
That night, while the 24th Marines resisted Japanese infiltration efforts,
we transferred the remaining fuel and ammunition to one of the pla-

**On the beach at Namur after the fight was over. Our potbellied cook,
Bill Downey, LEFT, was over forty and went back to the states after this
action. I am on the right. What a motley crew we seem to be,
now combat veterans all!**

toons for the next day's operation. That platoon moved into the lines just in time to assist in shattering the main Japanese counterattack. Later, near the end of the battle, the real ammo was landed.

Dick Schmidt came ashore the day Namur was declared secure, and his father, General Schmidt, who had landed on D-Day, was really pissed off at him for coming ashore after the fighting ended. Dick told me he was writing me up for a Navy Cross for what I had done. That was undoubtedly not called for, though, as we had just done what was expected of us. Then I found out that Colonel Jones was not kidding when he said he was going to have me arrested and charged. I learned later that Dick had gone to his dad and told him that this should not be allowed to happen. Apparently the general got both commanders together and told Dick to withdraw the decoration and Louie Jones to withdraw the charges, calling it even. So I was saved for the moment.

The LSD captain came ashore and Bob Reed and I showed him around. He told me the whole ship had listened to us on our frequency as we fought our way up Namur's west coast. In addition, he brought twenty gallons of ice cream ashore for us. We sent a helmet full to General Schmidt to show that we shared a little.

We first covered the side armor on our tanks with timber for the Roi operation, using two-inch planks of Douglas fir to keep Japanese magnetic mines from sticking to the hull when they assaulted the tanks. If they held the charges against the hull in a suicide attack, we calculated that the extra two inches of space between the hull and the charges would save the hull from penetration. A few crews placed planking on the front slope armor, but I did not require this measure. I got this idea from Leo Case on Guadalcanal, who had explained how the Japanese infantry tried to attack our tanks there.

I also took a number of auxiliary gasoline tanks from Jacque's Farm, intended for use on the light tanks but never used, and so never filled with gasoline. We bolted these on the rear of our tanks to carry water, which we gave out to the infantry operating with us, whom we obviously had a vested interest in keeping fit. We fitted bungs on each end of the water tanks so that they could refill their canteens during lulls in the fighting. Here was more evidence of the lack of unity in the battalion, as the other companies never picked up on our ideas and modifications. The tank-infantry telephone was the only idea they did adopt. That was another idea from Leo Case, who later became our battalion operations officer. Leo told me that communicating with the infantry

C Company snapshot on Roi-Namur, 1944. Sergeant Richard W. Moon Jr. (closest to camera) and Vincent F. Velota (no shirt, holding carbine). Note the wood planking on the side of the tank.

was a real tough problem, aggravated by the fact that our radios remained incompatible. Somebody in the company—perhaps it was the communications NCO, Gerry De Moss—came up with the idea of putting a field telephone with a spring-loaded retracting wire in a satchel on the left-rear fender. The phone had a direct line to the tank commander. Using the clock system for direction, with the front of the tank being twelve o'clock, the infantry would tell us what targets they saw and we then found them in our telescopic sights and engaged them. This was such an obviously good idea that the other companies quickly picked up on it. Later, the tanks we were issued had factory-installed phones.

Leaving Namur for Maui, we went on a long voyage aboard LST 222. Both marines and sailors called LSTs "large, slow targets." It was the flagship of an LST squadron, and had a commodore on board. The first night, we were still anchored in the lagoon when Jap bombers came over, hitting the island but not us. We got out of there the next day, not waiting for the other ships to load, and headed for Pearl Harbor. The ship's company was all reservists, including the officers. They were used to traveling in convoys and thus were unaccustomed to doing their own navigating. The trip took a long time, and the ship started to run out of food. I will never forget the cans of navy beans we ate for several days. We were on the verge of cutting back to two meals a day before we found our true position near Pearl Harbor. To make matters worse, the commodore turned out to be a real asshole. Our men were down in the hold with their tanks each day, playing around with their souvenirs and personal equipment. They were acting really salty, having fought and won their first battle, and they cursed a lot as they relived their experiences. The commodore sent for me, and when I reported to his cabin he told me the men were uncouth and that I was going to have to stop their swearing. I retorted that the men had just been in combat and were relaxing. How could he expect me to tell them not to swear? He said,

Sergeant Joe Bruno's tank at Roi, with a captured Japanese Type 94 light tank mounted on its back deck, is shown ready to embark for Maui after the battle. Members of the crew are, FROM LEFT: Jesse Mason Jr., loader; Petro H. "Creek" Kamilos, assistant driver; Frank G. Mathis, driver; Chris Kotila, gunner; and Bruno, platoon sergeant and tank commander.

Bob Reed (LEFT) and I pose together aboard LST-222 en route to the Hawaiian Islands after the Rio-Namur assaults in February, 1944.

"You'll do it or I'll have you locked up when we get to Pearl Harbor!" So I went down below, got the men together, and told them that I had been told to get them to stop swearing. I explained that if they did not, I was going to be locked up. Everybody laughed, but then they really tried to clean up their talk. I did not care at that point if I did get locked up or not. When we got to Pearl, the commodore got off, and the same ship took us to Maui after taking on some real food.

CHAPTER 7

Breaking the Japanese Barriers

Saipan and Tinian

We had the incredible good fortune in the 4th Marine Division to draw Maui as our home base. It remains to this day a lush, beautiful, tropical Pacific island, enchanting in its layout. During the war, it had two different kinds of economic activity: plantations and ranching. There was, of course, no tourism, and we frequented the commercial hotels, like the Pioneer Inn at Lahaina and the Maui Palms in Wailuku. The troops found great entertainment available in the towns as well. We had our own tank encampment on the beach, separate from the rest of the division. Nobody wanted the tanks tearing up the limited roads, which already had too much civilian and military traffic. That was just fine with us, and we worked and played on the beach, returning by truck to the division bivouac area at mealtime. We kept busy training and working in a few replacements. I eventually gave up my executive officer, Steve Horton, who took command of A Company. Bob Reed then became my exec, beginning what was going to be a great forty-year partnership and a true brotherhood. He had already shown me that he could handle his platoon well under fire, and he showed good sense and no apparent fear, although we all had our scares then and later.

Apparently, one of the more famous pictures to come out of the Roi-Namur assault was of a Japanese Type 94 light tank (a tankette, really) atop the engine deck of one of my company's tanks after the battle. We had taken one that we found relatively intact on Namur and used the company tank retriever (recovery vehicle) to hoist it onto the rear of an M4. We then carried it back to Maui with us on the LST. I do not remember who had the idea of taking this trophy first, but our maintenance people fixed it up on Maui and we ran around the tank training area in it and had a ball. We had to leave it behind when we went to Saipan, and never saw it again.

The frivolity on the beach reached new heights, however, in the strange case of the "Missing Hut." I could relate the story, but the best version came from the pen of Dick Turpin, one of my young enlisted

Sergeant Joe Bruno's tank is in the background with the Japanese Type 94 already loaded, and he and his crew are resting with another trophy, which we left behind. FROM LEFT IN THE REAR: Petro H. "Greek" Kamilos, assistant driver; Chris Kotila, gunner; and Jesse Mason Jr., loader. FROM LEFT IN FRONT: Bruno, platoon sergeant and commander, and Frank G. Mathis, assistant commander and driver.

marines, who later became the real estate editor for the *Los Angeles Times*. This is what he wrote in 1983:

■ ■ ■

Picture a group of rowdy Marines at a rest camp, newly returned from battle at Roi and Namur in the Kwajalein Atoll, unwinding, and drinking the infamous "green" beer of World War II. They made up C Company, 4th Tank Battalion, 4th Marine Division. The oldest was 31 and, of course, he was called "Pop."

One of the youngest had just remarked wistfully that it would be great to have a clubhouse on the beach where they could sit around, quaff the awful beer, tell lies, play cards and just rest. Sort of like the officers' club elsewhere. Well, it wasn't exactly "no sooner said than done" but it was close.

A tank company has many mechanical advantages over the foot troopers and C Company had a most unusual vehicle called a retriever, an all-purpose 30-ton Sherman tank with the capability and adaptability to become a land mine detector, a bulldozer or a crane of sorts. These assets were mostly the creation of an ingenious, rangy Texan, a gunnery sergeant.

A number of youths had spotted a small, pleasant looking hut not far from the beach tank park. It squatted there on its piers, probably the home of some field worker.

Its matted floor was about two feet above the ground. A cozy, thatched shelter that could instantaneously become a ready-made clubhouse, someone suggested. That did it.

Quickly, the retriever was rigged with grappling hooks and cables and rumbled its way up to the shelter. Its tentacles of steel embraced and lifted the flimsy dwelling off the piers and transported it to an open space In the middle of the tank farm, amid rousing cheers. Instant clubhouse!

The beer supply was immediately transferred to the cool interior of the shack and the party began. A record amount of the green beer was consumed in the ensuing hour or two before the field telephone nearby interrupted the revelry.

On the line was Capt. Robert M. Neiman, company commander, who told his executive officer, 1st Lt. Robert Reed, that he had been asked by the local chief of police if he knew the whereabouts of a stolen home. A resident of the area had just reported a missing house, Neiman told Reed, and added that the victim and the chief

The Japanese tankette we captured is shown here in use at our main motor pool area on Maui in 1944.

"wondered" if the nearby Marine tankers knew anything about such an unusual circumstance.

Neiman, always direct and succinct in all his orders, in battle or rest camp, told Reed, "Bob, I don't know anything about this man's house but if you do, get it the hell out of there. I'm bringing the chief and the man to the park in my jeep. We'll be there in 20 minutes!"

It had not been too difficult apparently for the victim to note that giant tank tracks led to his modest little abode and then toward the beach. There was his home, swarming with Marines.

Feverish activity followed Neiman's call. The retriever now donned its bulldozer blade, quickly dug and created a revetment, changed gears to hoist the shelter into the hole, pushed sand over the roof and backed away. The beer had been removed from the hut, sadly.

As the whine of Neiman's jeep came into earshot, scores of grinning young men idled away the beautiful Maui afternoon smoothing the sand under their feet. Some stomped about covering up any vestiges of the short-lived beer hall.

The Marines left the base shortly after. Those who were party to the impromptu club-building like to think that nature and the tides shortly uncovered the man's dwelling and restored his peace of mind.[1]

I made major soon after our arrival on Maui. I found out about it when General Schmidt's aides called me to his office at the main camp. When I arrived, they told me I was now a major and that the general wanted to pin the leaves on. Nobody made it a big deal, as I was the only one being promoted at the time. We had been talking for some time in the tank battalion about how we needed majors in command of tank companies because we often were detached from our battalion and assigned to infantry battalions or regiments where we had to deal with lieutenant colonels and colonels, correcting their misapprehensions about tanks. As field grade officers, our views would carry more weight with the other field grades. When I continued in command of C Company, I found the job really was much easier than it had been when I was a captain.

Our battalion received a complete set of M4A2 tanks, freshly delivered from the States. We went to work right away on a series of modifications.

Joe Dever, LEFT, and I, THIRD FROM LEFT, pose with a group from my company in front of the selective service office on Maui in Hawaii. We thought it was pretty funny at the time. Corporal John C. Shutt, the tall man to my left, usually served as our photographer.

We added a layer of sandbags over the rear engine compartment to add standoff space to protect against satchel charges that the enemy infantry might throw or place there. Then somebody figured out that the wood planks we had placed over the side armor would make perfect forms for pouring reinforced concrete. We welded short sections of reinforcing bar iron, sticking out perpendicular from the side armor, and also four sections of U-channels to the sides. Then we bolted the two-by-twelve wood planking on the ends of these sections and added a one-by-four bottom section, thus forming the outer part of the form. We then strung lengths of reinforcing bars horizontally between the angle-iron sections and mixed and poured the concrete. This gave us a two-inch layer of reinforced concrete covered with two-by-twelve wood planks. We thought that would be enough to stop any kind of antitank round the Japanese could fire at us. All we needed to replace sections blown away in combat was more lumber and concrete, which the Seabees always had in good supply. The only hitch in this modification came when we did it to the company dozer tank. It made the vehicle so heavy that it would swamp an LCM-3 landing craft. Sam Johnston, our company gunnery sergeant, added to all our vocabularies as he swore while chipping the concrete off the dozer tank with a pneumatic hammer.

In addition, we built internal racks for 75-mm ammunition, which we had run out of on Namur. With these, we could carry up to a hundred rounds of 75-mm ammo for the main gun. We packed plenty of extra machine-gun ammo as well, but we did not need any special racks for it because there were all kinds of nooks and crannies in which we could stuff ammo cans.

Equipment and tactical changes occurred often during the Pacific War. As soon as we became oriented to a new set of objectives, the situation would change. From attacking small, isolated Japanese garrisons on coral atolls like Tarawa and Kwajalein, the III and V Amphibious Corps turned to confronting much larger Japanese army units defending large Pacific islands with widely varied terrain. The Marianas formed Japan's inner island defense barrier, and a decisive battle fought there on land, at sea, and in the air would settle the fate of the empire.

Although U.S. Navy submarine and air interdiction delayed Japanese reinforcements and key fortification materials from reaching the Marianas in the early part of 1944, the garrisons already in place had artillery, tanks, and other heavy weapons. The U.S. invasion force, the largest yet assembled in the Pacific, would land on three large islands during Operation Forager: Saipan and nearby Tinian at the northern end of the archipelago, and Guam to the south. The V Amphibious Corps, using the 2d and 4th Marine Divisions with the army's 27th Infantry Division in reserve, planned to take Saipan first, then turn on nearby Tinian. The III Amphibious Corps (formerly the I Marine Amphibious Corps during the Solomons campaign), would land the 3d Marine Division and the 1st Provisional Marine Brigade (4th and 22d Marines) on Guam, with the 77th Infantry Division, held initially in Hawaii, in reserve.

We stopped at Eniwetok en route to Saipan. The island was secure and had a makeshift officer's club on the beach as well as an NCO club. We sat on this gorgeous beach swimming and drinking beer. It was a great day, especially compared to riding on the ship, which was always darkened at night, and wondering if any Japanese submarines were around.

We had good luck and we accomplished a lot of good training in preparation for D-Day on Saipan: June 15, 1944. In all amphibious operations, each unit is given a place to land and a time. Ours was a long dock with a dredged channel alongside it at Charan-Kanoa, the sugar town, located in the center of the 4th Marine Division's landing area. A concrete ramp also extended out into the channel. Some guy at division headquarters who should have known better decided that that was where the tanks should land, since it would be easier for the Landing Craft, Medium (LCMs), to off-load us there than go in over the reef. We in the tank battalion remained skeptical, however, thinking that it was the one place the Japanese guns would be zeroed in on for sure.

I decided that I for one would *not* land there. Instead, I sent a reconnaissance team carrying walkie-talkies set to my company tactical net in with the first wave of infantry, with the mission of finding a good place for us to land. One of the other companies tried the channel and got shot up. As our LCMs began to follow the waves of amtracs toward the beach, I encountered a navy boat carrying underwater demolition team (UDT) swimmers coming out of the beach area. They had been working on taking out the underwater obstacles. I recognized one of the officers in the boat. He had been one of the marine instructors for my officer candidate class. I hailed the craft from my LCM and jumped over as it pulled alongside. "Is there a place we can land without obstacles?" I asked. He pointed out an area where he said there were few if any

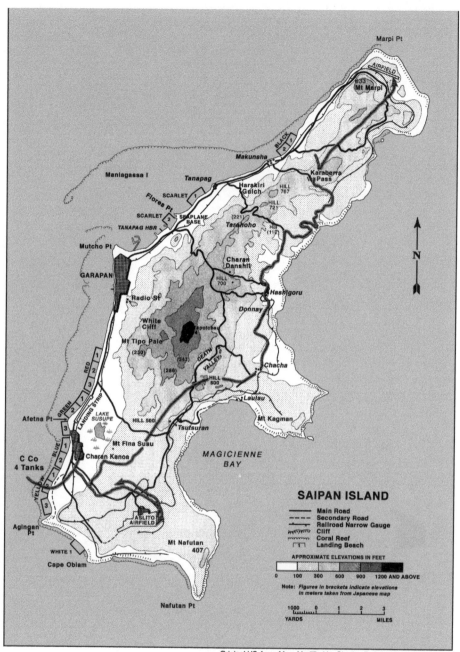

SAIPAN ISLAND

Main Road
Secondary Road
Railroad Narrow Gauge
Cliff
Coral Reef
Landing Beach

APPROXIMATE ELEVATIONS IN FEET

0   100   300   600   900   1200 AND ABOVE

Note: *Figures in brackets indicate elevations in meters taken from Japanese map*

1000   0   1   2   3
YARDS   MILES

Marpi Pt
AIRFIELD
933 Mt Marpi
BLACK 2
Makunsha
Karaberra Pass
Maniagassa I
Tanapag
Harakiri Gulch
HILL 767
SCARLET 1
Florea Pt
HILL 721
SCARLET 2
SEAPLANE BASE
TANAPAG HBR
(221)
Tarahoho
HILL (11)
Mutcho Pt
Charan Danshii
GARAPAN
HILL 700
Hashigoru
Radio St
Donnay
White Cliff
Tapotchau
Mt Tipo Pale
(230)
(343)
DEATH VALLEY
Chacha
(286)
HILL 600
RED 1
RED 2
RED 3
Laulau
Afetna Pt
GREEN 2
HILL 500
Mt Kagman
LANDING STRIP
LAKE SUSUPE
GREEN 3
Tsutsuran
BLUE 1
Mt Fina Susu
MAGICIENNE BAY
C Co 4 Tanks
BLUE 2
Charan Kanoa
YELLOW 2
YELLOW 3
ASLITO AIRFIELD
Agingan Pt
WHITE 1
Mt Nafutan 407
Cape Obiam
Nafutan Pt

N

Original US Army Map, Modified by Charles B. Ash and W. Stephen Hill obstacles and told me we would have no problem getting in over the reef to the beach. I could not see for sure, but just then there was a huge explosion and a column of water rose into the air, I guess from one of their demolition charges. "See that?" he asked. "Just go in there and you'll have no problem as far as obstacles are concerned." By then, the Japanese had taken interest in our boats coming together and started to lob some shells our way. I jumped back in the LCM and we got the hell out of there, as did the swimmers' boat.

We headed for the reef in our usual formation of a company column of platoons, each platoon on line, fifty yards between each vehicle and between each platoon. The announced timing for the landing was shot, but we were going in. Once on the reef, we put some men from my company headquarters in the water. They swam ahead wearing fins and goggles, trailing toilet paper behind them to mark the way. All the crews had to do was follow the toilet paper as it unrolled and they would reach the beach. Once there, I found one of the recon teams waiting, saying that one of the infantry battalion commanders was asking for our support. They guided us five hundred yards down the beach to the battalion's command post. The mission was to recon Charan-Kanoa and the mill area behind the pier.

It was weird. We drove through the town buttoned up. We did not know what we would find, looking through our periscopes. There was a big mill and a dozen blocks of workers' houses, and although we shot up a few suspicious places, we found no sign of enemy troops. What we did not know was that the Japanese had left a forward observer up in the smokestack to call artillery in on us. We reported that we had encountered no resistance to the infantry, and they came through all right. However, the artillery continued to pour down on us from the Japanese positions up on the ridge overlooking the landing area, and there was little cover for us.

We started to advance inland toward the ridge, but one of the first things that happened was that we encountered the swamp known as Lake Susupe and Bob Reed's tank got stuck. Shells were falling all around us. Each of our tanks had a coiled cable on the front end and a hitch on the rear. I jumped out of my tank and attached the cable to the hitch on Reed's tank and had Charles B. Ash, my driver, back up until the cable was taut. Then I got back in and radioed Reed what we were doing, so that he could reverse his tracks while we were pulling backward on the cable. We were able to get him out of there that way. Later,

I remember hearing calls on my radio from a navy gunfire support ship, and then a call from an observer, but they could not hear each other. I ended up relaying for them, hoping that the observer would get one of the ships to fire on the Japanese artillery.

We did not get very far that night and had to pull back to rearm. Dick Schmidt joined us under our tank for the night. We would dig a slit trench, drive a tank over it and then take some of the sandbags off the engine cover and put them on the front, and between the bogey wheels. Then we dismounted one of the machine guns, thus making a nice pillbox. We really needed it what with all the artillery fire, both direct from the ridgeline covering the road inland, as well as indirect fire from the rest of the island.

So ended our first day on Saipan. Dick's father had ordered him to go ashore at Saipan, and when we ran into him, he seemed glad to have found us, as he was not having a good day. From what he told us that night, I think that he suffered much from trying to live up to what he thought was expected of him as an only son. He never functioned as the tank battalion's tactical commander. He simply acted as an administrative head of three companies separately attached to infantry regiments. The other divisional tank battalion commanders, to my knowledge, took tactical control of their battalions in the field after their tanks had landed with the regiments on D-day of any assault. It never happened in the 4th Tank Battalion, but it certainly became routine in the 1st, when Jeb Stuart was running it, and in the 6th with Bob Denig, and probably in the 3d. I know this is how Rip Collins ran the 5th Tank Battalion.

■   ■   ■

I received a real scare on Saipan. It was the only time that I ever shivered and shook. It happened on the third night. Fighting was heavy initially, and we would bring the tanks back to the beach each night to rearm and refuel, but mostly to rearm. The basic theory was for tanks to stay out of the fighting at night and prepare for action at first light. We always came back to the beach, set up one or two hundred yards inland, and dug in, using the tanks to cover our trenches as I described earlier. One guy in each tank remained on watch in the commander's hatch, and the rest of the crews went into their holes to sleep.

That night, Tokyo radio was playing its *Zero Hour* program, on which Tokyo Rose appeared. The Japanese would play big band or Bing Crosby songs, and then Rose would tell us we were risking our lives, getting killed by their soldiers and airmen, while back home our wives and girlfriends were going out with guys who were 4-F and things like that. This was a big laugh, but we listened because the music was good. The Philippine Sea naval battle began that day, which we did not know ashore, and all the ships were gone. Rose was saying that the marines on Saipan had been abandoned and that hundreds of planes would soon bomb and destroy us. Of course, the fighting was tough, the navy was apparently gone, and many of us still remembered the navy's defeat at Savo Island near Guadalcanal and the abandonment of the 1st Marine Division there for a while. Still, we laughed it off.

Somehow, though, it must have stuck in my mind. Not long after her broadcast, we went to sleep beside the tank because it was hotter than hell. The next thing I knew, one of our sentries was yelling, "Condition red, condition red!" I was dog tired, but I pulled myself under the tank. A little later there were some big explosions, and I thought, Holy mackerel! Tokyo Rose was right: a big Jap air armada is dropping stuff all over us. I was still half-asleep, half in a bad dream, and I started shaking like crazy. The booming continued, and I finally pulled myself together and crawled out so I could see what was happening to my company. I found my crew sound asleep by the tank, apparently without a care in the world. Then I realized that no bombs had fallen, it was just our own artillery firing. Under the cover of darkness, an army 155-mm battery had come in and set up about 150 yards behind us. They were making a big racket and in my haze of sleep, I had thought they were Japanese planes. The "red alert" had been for a single plane that flew overhead, and the army had provided the sound effects that had so badly shaken me. I never did tell the guys how shaky I had been while they were sleeping.

■　■　■

Not far away was the road from Charan-Kanoa to Aslito Airfield that we would take as we advanced farther east. This was a more satisfying day than the first had been. The 24th or 25th Regimental Combat Team (RCT), so-called when ashore as a reinforced regiment, was ordered by division to go down the road and cross the ridge to the airfield on the other side. We were assigned to that RCT and led the way in column down the road to the airfield with the infantry following us in amtracs. This plan was doomed, because we were going into a heavily defended area with our infantry riding in the lightly armored amtracs with their open tops.

My platoon leaders, Reed, and I had taken our tanks to the command post (CP) meeting with the RCT commander, and parked about

Tanks and Infantry move out on Tinian, 1944.

seventy-five yards away from an enlarged shell hole that served as the regimental CP. The Japanese saw the indications of our movement or the group of radio antennae at the CP, and shells started to fall, breaking up the meeting and killing one of the battalion commanders, Lt. Col. Maynard C. Schultz. This was not an auspicious beginning, but the plans had been made by then and the orders given.

I had my watch pinned to my shirt (to this day I cannot wear a wristwatch because it produces a terrible rash), and as I approached my tank after the meeting, *wham,* a shell hit right beside it, knocking me down. After I got up and jumped in the tank, I took stock of myself and found that my watch was gone. That one had come close!

Anyway, we lined up and maneuvered down the road, coordinating by radio. Behind us wound a long column of half-track mounted 75-mm guns, armored amtracs, and amtracs filled with infantry. Up ahead, the road cut through the top of the ridge, from which the Japanese had been bombarding the beachhead. The cut through the ridge was a couple of hundred yards long, about twenty or thirty yards wide, and its sides were about ten feet high. We approached in a company column with platoons in column. I was first into the cut, and it was swarming with Japanese. Thank God, they had no antitank weapons—just machine guns and mortars. We engaged them for an hour or so, shooting the hell out of them as we moved slowly through.

While the fight was going on, I looked up the road and saw a single Japanese infantryman standing in the center, setting up a tripod. I was sure that he must have an antitank weapon of some sort. Why else would he be setting up in the middle of the road? Rick Haddix, my gunner (later to lose a leg as a tank commander on Iwo), was shooting up some target on the left side and I tried to get his attention, but he did not hear me over the intercom. I kicked him several times and he finally turned around and I just pointed in the direction I wanted him to fire. We both sighted over there in time to see that the guy had set up a heavy machine gun. Haddix got him right away with his coax and then triggered the main gun. I thought what a futile gesture for that soldier. The company eventually worked its way through the cut, almost certainly killing more Japanese soldiers that day than we did on any other during the war.

There was one problem: the amtracs did not follow us, and we were alone on the far side. We could see the airfield in the distance. The road we were on dropped off the ridgeline, but remained about six feet above the flat land below. I figured there was a bog on either side. Given Reed's experience at Lake Susupe, I decided to stay on the road and head for the airfield. A couple of miles ahead, a railroad track crossed the road and led straight into the airstrip. We had just begun to follow that line when the rear tank was knocked out by a direct hit from one of the artillery rounds dropping around us. The tank commander, a corporal, was killed, and several crewmen wounded. G. M. English, who was bringing up the rear, told me there were still no friendly infantry in sight, so I decided to sweep the airfield quickly and return to the road cut.

The marines had occupied the ridgeline and spread out, mopping up the Japanese lines. My column of tanks was now spread out over several hundred yards. We got the wounded crewmen into tanks and then picked up their tank commander's body. I told English to push the wrecked tank off the road with his tank, and he promptly complied. I still suspected the ground alongside the road was too soft. It probably was okay. It looked like a harvested sugarcane field, but I did not want to chance it, especially since no infantry were with us.

The artillery continued to fire at us as we headed back up the road, and indirectly at the marines up on the ridge. We fired back, knocking out several guns—maybe a half-dozen of the thirty or so that were there. We rejoined the marines on the ridge after withdrawing through a sustained barrage. There I learned that the amtrac-mounted infantry had failed to keep up with us because of their light protection, just as I had anticipated. Then they had to stop and clear the ridge to either side of the road cut. That had occupied the rest of their day.

The tank that had been knocked out was about a thousand yards inside the Japanese lines. We did not want it captured and used against us, so I sent Sam Johnston back with my tank, "Ill Wind," to destroy it. It took about twenty rounds of armor-piercing ammo to set it on fire. After Johnston returned, we headed back to the beach to rearm and refuel.

■　■　■

We checked the cane fields the next day and found them dry enough to cross. The Japanese, meanwhile, had dug in with artillery, mortars, and machine guns facing us across two thousand yards of open ground. It was June 17, one of the best days we would ever have in C Company.

My M4A2 medium tank "Ill Wind" is shown here advancing with infantry through a sugarcane field on Tinian in the summer of 1944. National Archives photo, courtesy Oscar E. Gilbert.

There was no way for the infantry to cross. Colonel Louie Jones, the 23d RCT commander, and I decided to let the tanks lead at first. I wanted maximum speed in case they had any antitank (AT) guns of any size. We started our engines at around eight or nine in the morning and moved out in a shallow V formation, with me in the center. We picked up speed and the next thing I knew, a sheet of fire flashed through our tank and everything went blank. I came to in a daze and saw the rest of my crew passed out, but the tank was still moving toward the enemy. I had no intercom and we had no power. I managed to kick the guys awake and stop. I waved a nearby tank over as I dismounted from my tank and jumped aboard. A large artillery shell must have hit our tank, stunning us and knocking out the electrical circuits that operated the turret and radio. A diesel engine needs no electrical source, so the tank had continued to move! We could not fight it without power, though, and I had to keep up with the company. The rest of my crew clambered aboard and I sent the crew of the tank I had commandeered to the rear. I do not remember whose tank I took over, but we had gone only went a little farther when, *Boom!* We had hit a mine. Once again we were stunned. The radio was out and we had a broken track. I waved to the nearest tank that he was next. I remember a guy on that tank pointing to the tank I was in and shouting a warning about magnetic mines, but it was the tank with Corporal Schutt, our company photographer, as a crewman. He had left his film can on the tank when he jumped off to make room for us. This was my third tank of the day, and we had another five hundred yards to go. The artillery was supposed to fire on the enemy lines as we approached, but it failed to happen. The plan was for us to button up and attack through air bursts like we had practiced at Camp Pendleton, but it did not happen then or any other time in the Pacific War, to my knowledge. So we went in without fire support but we wound up having a field day similar to what Leo Case had at the Tenaru River battle on Guadalcanal. We took out the Japanese mortar, artillery, and machine-gun positions, plus a lot of their infantry. Our own infantry soon arrived and took over, mopping up what remained of the defenses. We had made it all the way across Saipan and were on a cliff overlooking the eastern shore. We lost only two of the fourteen tanks with which we had gone into action that day.

■　■　■

We saw only limited action during the rest of the Saipan campaign because there was not much we could do to help the infantry in the center of the island. The infantry wound up in a terrible fight in the mountainous interior. One day, though, about two or three days later, we accompanied an infantry battalion down a narrow canyon road to Cha Cha village. The terrain widened around the village and we spread out. It seemed deserted. I jumped out of my tank to look around and perhaps meet with the infantry battalion commander. I was maybe four or five feet from one of the houses when Bob Reed suddenly called out, "For Christ's sake," and pulled me away as a grenade rolled out from one of the stilt houses. The grenade hit my foot, but it did not explode. There was a Jap underneath the house. We jumped back in our tanks and blew that house up. Then we blew up all the other houses, just to make sure.

We saw more of Dick Schmidt's policy of leaving the companies alone on Saipan, even after he came ashore with the battalion staff and set up his headquarters. The companies stayed with the infantry regiments they had been assigned to in training for the operation until the end. After we crossed the island, we went north on the east coast, and crossed again from east to west at the north end. Our tanks came to the edge of a cliff overlooking the northwest part of the island and saw a coastal plain. I called Colonel Jones at his CP a mile to the rear and he told me to take the tanks over the cliff. I could not believe it. He kept ordering me down the cliff. I called Schmidt, but he was several miles to the rear. When I asked Dick if I was under Jones's command or his, he replied that technically he was in charge of the tank units. I suggested he tell Jones that. "I can't do that," he replied. Then I said, "But you aren't ordering me over the cliff right?" He replied that I had assumed correctly. "Well, good then," I said. "I won't have to do it."

I wanted to get down there just as much as Jones did, of course, but I wanted a safe way down. I crossed over to the right flank and ran into a 2d Division unit. After finding a good place to get down to the plain, I ran across one of the 2d Division regimental commanders. I cannot remember his name now, but I told him what I was doing.[2] This was another one of the times when it was good to be a major rather than a captain. I introduced myself and asked if he knew Colonel Jones. "You mean loudmouthed Louie?" he replied, in a deep southern drawl. I pointed out my former position and explained that we could not get down the cliff from there. I then asked if he would he let me go through his position and advise Colonel Jones that it was okay? "Sure," he said. "Can you get Louie on the radio for me?" I raised the regiment on the radio and he talked to Jones, saying: "Louie where are you hiding?

Come up and see this cliff. Your tanks are here, but they can't get down, so I'm going to let them go through my position. I just wanted to let you know that."

And that is just what we did, taking an infantry company along with us on our tanks. That was the last of my squabbles with Louie Jones. Maybe after this incident he figured out that I was generally on the right track as far as tank employment went.

After we descended from the escarpment, civilians began jumping off the cliffs. This happened mainly in the 2d Division's sector, but you could not miss it. We saw it happen from a distance.

■   ■   ■

For our next landing in the Marianas, on Tinian, we took advantage of air observation. This may have been the first use of air observers with tanks, which later became part of doctrine. We had about three weeks to prepare for the Tinian operation. We would cross over from Saipan in a vessel called a Landing Craft, Tank (LCT), instead of using ships. It was like an LCM, but it could carry two or three tanks. On Saipan we had experienced problems crossing cane fields that had not been harvested. The open fields were bad enough, offering clear fields of fire to anyone dug in on the far side. But you could only see a couple of feet ahead in the unharvested fields. It was a weird thing, attacking in a tank and not being able to see anything. You might as well be buttoned up without a periscope or anything else to look through. We spent a lot of time trying to figure out how we might overcome this. Tinian looked almost totally flat, and it was covered with unharvested cane fields. Talking about it in the company, we decided to get help from the observation planes attached to division headquarters. I knew the squadron commander, so I explained our problem to him and suggested we try practicing. We put a tank officer in his plane with a radio set on my frequency. We went to the field on a training day and crossed a typical cane field on Saipan. The plane circled overhead as our observer called out clock directions to simulated Jap positions. The pilot, seeing how we trained our guns, corrected our "fire" and walked the tanks through the zone. As it turned out, planes were not always available on Tinian, but we made good use of them when they were. Fortunately there was not as much resistance on Tinian, so it did not make a great deal of difference. It was still a good idea. We employed this tactic before Kunishi Ridge on Okinawa in a somewhat similar situation, and Jeb Stuart used it as part of the justification for the Bronze Star I was awarded there.

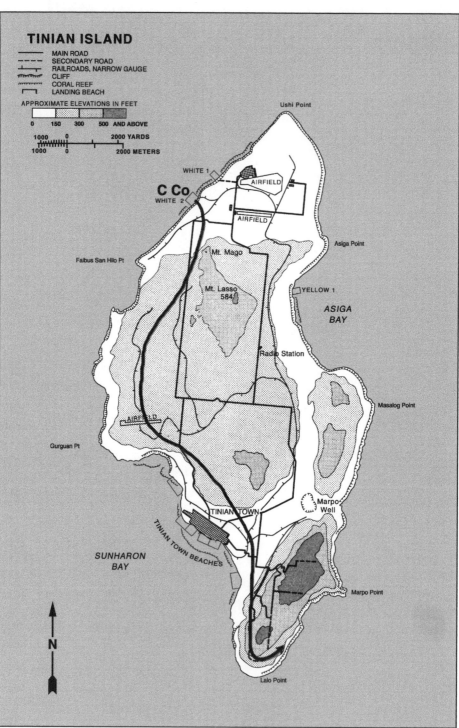

TINIAN ISLAND

— MAIN ROAD
- - - SECONDARY ROAD
+ RAILROADS, NARROW GAUGE
CLIFF
CORAL REEF
LANDING BEACH

APPROXIMATE ELEVATIONS IN FEET

0   150   300   500 AND ABOVE

1000   0   2000 YARDS
1000   0   2000 METERS

Ushi Point

WHITE 1
C Co
WHITE 2

AIRFIELD

AIRFIELD

Asiga Point

Faibus San Hilo Pt

Mt. Mago

Mt. Lasso
584

YELLOW 1

ASIGA
BAY

Radio Station

Masalog Point

AIRFIELD

Gurguan Pt

Marpo
Well

Marpo Point

TINIAN TOWN

SUNHARON
BAY

TINIAN TOWN BEACHES

N

Lalo Point

Original US Army map, modified by Charles B. Ash and W. Stephen Hill

The division's tactical commanders also made an aerial reconnaissance of Tinian. This had to be the first and only time in the Pacific War that Marine Corps unit commanders down to tank company level had this opportunity before an amphibious assault. We went up in a Grumman TBM Avenger and flew up and down the island along the coast, relatively unmolested by Japanese antiaircraft fire. Instead, the Japanese dueled with the flak suppression planes, P-47 Thunderbolts that the army had brought to Saipan. Each was armed with eight .50-caliber machine guns, and they provided quite an impressive show. We watched the Japanese tracers arc upward, fighting a losing battle against the heavy volume of U.S. tracers homing in on their positions.

With our maps in hand, we could see the differences in the actual terrain and also spot areas where we could maneuver most easily. We marked all these on our maps as we circled the island twice. We thus had the advantage of real familiarity with the terrain before we landed. I went into action knowing where tanks could operate on the island and where the terrain might prove difficult for us. Furthermore, I had pinpointed routes that would allow us to bypass the difficult spots.

The landing on Tinian was made over a coral shelf, not a beach. The narrow landing sites gave us the rare and priceless advantage of surprise, however, and the assault force went in unopposed for the moment. None of the letters I sent home have survived the years since, save one that was published in our local paper. It still reads well today and summarizes the unusual experience we had on D-Day:

It had been decided to land one division at a time on Tinian because of the narrowness of the beaches we would use. Whereas on Saipan the landing was made with two divisions abreast, on Tinian, the Fourth Division was to land on D-Day and the Second Division on the same benches on D plus 1. Within the Fourth Division it was decided that the 23rd Marines would land in reserve behind the two assault regiments. My company was attached to the 23rd and this would be the first time we would land in reserve rather than in assault.

The 23rd was landing in reserve this time because it only had about 2,000 men left out of 6,000, whereas the other regiments were at half strength. Now the plan was that if either of the two assault regiments received very heavy casualties at the beach, the

23rd would pass through them on landing and the regiment that it passed through would go into reserve. If neither assault regiment suffered too much at the beach, the 23rd would assemble after it landed, at a previously designated area to the right of the right assault regiment, and prepare to attack along the division right flank. That latter plan was the one put into use.

My tanks landed with the elements of the 23rd. When we reached our assembly area it was still in front of the front lines. And as it later turned out, apparently most of the Japs who weren't killed on the beaches, fled into this area and set up their guns. Our assembly area was very heavily wooded, which meant we couldn't see more than a few yards in any direction but did have good concealment from the hills ahead of us.

As the various elements of the 23rd were arriving in the area, I got out of my tank and went on reconnaissance for the forthcoming attack with one of the battalion commanders. During all this time, we received scattered sniper fire, which really didn't bother anyone.

But as I returned from my reconnaissance, our whole area fell under extremely heavy machine gun fire from at least a half dozen guns that were firing from very close, practically point blank range. Well, there we were, we were landed in reserve and getting the Hell kicked out of us. We hadn't had time to dig in. We were all bunched up. We had been led to believe that we were relatively safe. But we were definitely not safe. Naturally everybody hugged the deck. I was hugging the ground behind a wheel of my radio jeep. When the shooting started, I was not in my tank, a fact that I cursed over and over during the next hour. I was in a radio jeep from which I had intended to control the tanks during the attack.

During the next hour, men were killed all through our area. The thing almost seems funny now, the fact that we were theoretically still in reserve, but it was deadly serious then. The situation was definitely bad. No one could lift himself even a few inches off the ground without being shot.

The machine guns were right in amongst us, but due to the heavy underbrush we couldn't see them. Men were being killed all around me. My jeep soon was full of holes. Every time I'd lift my head a little to try to talk into my radio transmitter (to get some tanks up there) my jeep would get a few more holes in it.

However, I did talk to some of my tanks over the radio. I told them what I wanted them to do. But most of the tank crews were pinned down outside of their tanks. They (the tanks) were only about 50 years behind me and there was too much noise to yell that far.

Finally, my men were able, one by one, to get into their tanks. Then, following my instructions, they came up and swept through the area immediately in front of us. They knocked out some of the guns but couldn't find them all. Most of the firing ceased, however.

It was getting dark now, and all thought of an attack (by us) was out for that day. But now we were able at least to rapidly organize and dig in for the night. After the infantry was squared away, I pulled my tanks in behind them and we dug in (me under my tank). We knew it would be a hectic night and would probably include a Nip counterattack. It did![3]

The Japanese realized we had landed at the other end of the island and their commander decided to attack us banzai-style. The Japanese counterattack that night saved a lot of marines' lives and made the next day's effort easy. They conveniently charged right into our fire. They came in with our infantry all set up and alerted. They even had a few tanks, which the marine infantry completely wiped out without our help. Some of the enemy troops rode on the tanks, officers waving their sabers, as they approached our lines. We watched the action from our reserve positions and took no part in the fight as our artillery lit up the night and the troops manning the lines poured fire into the attackers. My only casualty was Art Carlson, who lost his leg to a wound during the assembly area fight, although the Japanese did throw a lot of artillery our way. That is one reason the rest of the island put up so little resistance. The enemy had shot their bolt. Their tactics were crazy, accomplishing nothing. They had no advantage at night. Our ships and mortars put up hundreds of illumination rounds and we easily beat off their attacks. The Japanese did not try that at Iwo or Okinawa, which is one reason why those battles proved to be a lot tougher. There were a lot of local counterattacks in those last battles, but nothing on a mass level like on the other Marianas islands.

■   ■   ■

G. M. English called in on our fourth day on Tinian to report that he had just come across the largest cache of booze he had ever seen. "What do you want me to do?" he asked. I told him to load it in the tanks, and he said he had already done that. I told him to make sure nobody opened any of it or I would shoot him. Two days later, when we went into reserve for twenty-four hours, I assembled the troops at our bivouac site and distributed the stuff. I told them to enjoy it, as we would be going into action the next day. We always said that the Japanese should have put out poisoned booze, as we would have drunk it and they would have won. I had just killed a quart bottle of Asahi beer and S. Sgt. De Moss was standing next to me holding a half-pint of rum, looking at it gratefully, when a jeep rolled up and out hopped a messenger with a dispatch from, division: "Two Marines have died from drinking poisoned Japanese liquor if you run across any, destroy it immediately, because they have apparently poisoned [the booze]." Our worst nightmare had apparently come true. I looked at De Moss and told him to hand me his booze, whereupon I smashed it against the side of my tank. He looked shocked, absolutely frozen in disbelief, so I showed him the message. He read it and said, "Thanks!" We quickly reassembled everybody. Some of the men had started drinking, but they had not had much. "We won't destroy it," I said. "Just recollect it and we'll hold it until we can confirm this. When I get back, we'll either redistribute it or destroy it." I went to division and learned the true story. It seems that some of the Japanese farmers kept their insecticide in old sake bottles in their barns. Apparently a couple of guys had come across some wine bottles containing insecticide and died after they drank them. That was enough for me. As soon as I returned, we gave out most of the bottles again. There was plenty left, even though I had broken De Moss's. Among that store of booze were two bottles of Suntory scotch. I killed one bottle with two marines and saved the other bottle to drink with my Dad if I made it back to the states. De Moss ran a bar after the war in Indianapolis, and Chilly Newman, our admin clerk, used to go to the Kentucky Derby with him. So I would see "Diddy-dot" whenever I went to 4th Division reunions, for which Chilly was a great organizer. I will always remember the expression on De Moss's face when I smashed that bottle of rum.

■ ■ ■

The next day, we began running down the island from north to south, never really stopping. At one point we ran ahead of the 3d Battalion, 25th Marines, commanded by Lt. Col. Justice M Chambers. Division apparently had in mind a sort of a reconnaissance in force. Chambers had asked for a tank company and we got the job. Anyway, we went forward, starting after dusk, and advanced a couple of miles along the west coast, about a thousand yards inland. We did not encounter anything, so we dug in for the rest of the night. We were laying wire from the tanks to Chambers's CP, when we came under shell fire—not from the Japanese, but from a U.S. destroyer offshore that had seen our movement well behind the known Japanese lines and opened up on us. Somebody on our side quickly fired flare pistols into the air, giving the proper signal, so our casualties were not heavy. Chambers made up some songs that night to get everybody's minds off the tension by challenging the men to add a stanza, and so forth. I thought he was quite a leader, being able to defuse the situation so easily.

While we were there we sent some of our tanks out at night, although we just followed the infantry and never got into a fight. It was a rare experience. As dawn approached, Chambers got word to wait for the rest of the regiment and then resume the advance. Shortly after that we approached Tinian Town, which was not visible at first because of the woods surrounding it. Coming upon it from the back we were impressed by the fortifications the Japanese had built there. They had been abandoned by that point, and we were glad we had not landed there.

Chambers was nicknamed "Jumping Joe." He was a tall, lanky guy, who stood about six-foot-four inches tall. He did not walk, but rather jumped or lurched. He was the only infantry battalion commander I ever encountered in the war who was a reservist. He had been in Heinie Miller's Washington, D.C., reserve battalion. He was severely wounded on Iwo, and received the Medal of Honor for his heroism there. After the war, he became a lobbyist for foreign governments, including a lot of new Third World governments. Suzy and I used to have dinner with Joe and his wife after the war on our frequent visits to the D.C. area. Joe was a driving force behind establishing the 4th Marine Division memorial park on Maui, although Chilly Newman ultimately did it. That park is now a very big thing there.

■ ■ ■

By the last day of operations on Tinian, the Japanese had been forced into a pocket at one end of the island. There was high ground with a sheer drop of a couple of hundred feet to a shelf that was a hundred yards wide and several hundred long. Then there was another drop of about 150 to two hundred feet down to the ocean, with lots of rocks and surf at the base. We arrived on top of this stepped cliff and discovered a lot of caves along the upper shelf. Marines stood all over the top, and

I pulled my tanks off to the side so that we could fire down into the caves. Division had taken the Japanese manager of the big sugar mill in town prisoner and was using him to plead with the civilians to surrender, promising that they would receive good treatment and so forth. We were all holding our fire. Major General Clifton B. Cates, our new division commander, instructed his staff to let the Japanese manager try to talk the Japanese into surrendering. We knew that both soldiers and civilians were hiding in the caves because there was no other place where they could be. Although the man talked a very long time, nobody came out.

Finally, after about half an hour, we saw a family come out onto the shelf: a man and a woman with three or four children. They slowly walked from a cave out to the middle of the shelf. The guy with the bullhorn, we learned later, was telling them how to climb out of there. They formed a little circle and I thought they were preparing to surrender. They seemed to be straightening their clothes and general appearance. After that they formed a little circle and bowed to each other. We figured that they would try to climb up, but then there were puffs of smoke around them. They were blowing themselves up with grenades. Other families came out and began doing the same thing. Then a lady came running out at full speed with a child under each arm. She ran all the way to the edge of the cliff and threw the infants into the ocean below. Then she jumped herself. Similar scenes were acted out for a while, and then Japanese troops began to come out slowly and started killing themselves. When no more civilians came for a while, General Cates decided that there were no more inside and gave the command to open fire. We blasted the caves, firing a lot of rounds through the openings that were clearly visible. When no one else came out, a number of marines went down and went over the dead, looking for survivors and anything of intelligence value.

■ ■ ■

Tinian is always referred to as the "perfect landing," which it was. We had very few casualties and we wiped the enemy out within a few days. Our tanks were used effectively, and it was good terrain for them. In addition, the air recce we did gave us the benefit of knowing the lay of the island in advance. This was the one assault where we really surprised the Japanese with our choice of landing sites. On Iwo, it was obvious that we had to land at the little end near Suribachi. But at Tinian, we landed where we were not expected and it proved to be a complete shock to the enemy. The beach was very narrow, but it was a hell of a lot better when we could sneak ashore. I did have the tense experiences of the night counterattack and the close call that first afternoon with the Japanese machine guns at our bivouac site. We always liked banzai charges because the Japanese took so many casualties and we had fewer enemy troops to dig out later the hard way. The Japanese eventually learned to fight with greater tenacity from their fixed positions, which caused us no end of problems on Peleliu, Iwo, and Okinawa.

The 4th Marine Division again went back to Maui and our island paradise on the beach where we had our tank park. While we rode the ship back, the company officers asked me if we could rent a place to live outside of the division's tent camp. After thinking about it, I agreed to this idea, provided that one officer always remained at the camp and I would not be that officer! English and Gil Bradley eventually found a beautiful and exotic cliff house, built in the shape of a ship by a retired Danish ship captain, with the prow pointed at the sea. It stood halfway up Mount Haleakala, near Kula, and offered a splendid view of the ocean. It had several bedrooms, a bar, nice living areas, a jukebox, and an electrically heated water system. It was simply perfect. We had many dinners and once threw a big battalion party there. We invited all the girls we could find, including some nurses from nearby Kula Sanitarium. The senior nurse, I think, took a dim view of what was going on at our cliff house, especially when we failed to invite her to the party.

While we were on Maui this time, we did some experiments in an effort to make a flail tank. The flail was a copy of an army attempt one of us had read about in either the *Armored Force Journal* or *Infantry Journal*, as I recall. The article showed a tank with a rotating chain mounted in front that was used to beat a path through minefields. I discussed this with my officers and NCOs and we agreed to try it as we thought that we were eventually going to encounter mines and there were not always engineers available to handle the mine-clearing job. A few key NCOs, including Sam Johnston and the chief maintenance NCO, S. Sgt. Ray Shaw, built it. Sam and Ray used a salvaged dozer tank. The dozer's arms held a truck axle and differential with a drive shaft connected to the hull front and a jeep transmission connected to the tank drive shaft just inside it. They welded chains to the rotating axle. After a lot of fooling around we were ready.

This is the flail tank used for mine-clearing operations that we
built on Maui. It had a semiarmored differential casing.
Gy. Sgt. Johnston is at the controls.

Here's another view of the flail tank with the fully armored
differential casing on Maui in November, 1944. Tech. Sgt. Shaw
is standing by the turret.

Division authorized the engineers to lay a live minefield, and the flail tank detonated several as it beat a thirty- or forty-yard path. The only damage to the rig was a fragment that came at an odd angle past the armor plate bolted to the underside of the differential and holed it. We made a full armor wrap for that part, and no more damage resulted when we tried it again. Dick Schmidt let me inform Cates of our success and ask for an exhibition so other units could see it. All the brass on the island was coming, not just the senior officers from the division.

The next morning, Sam Johnston was drunk as a skunk from celebrating overnight, but he still insisted on driving the tank. It took three guys to haul him off to his tent. Maurice MacMahon was the only guy in the company big enough to put Johnston in his tent and keep him there while another man performed the demonstration, flailing through the minefield.

Here I am enjoying a break at the Puunene Athletic Club pool on Maui after our return from the Saipan and Tinian landings.

Author's collection.

Me, LEFT, and my executive officer, Bob Reed, with the company-made flail tank used for mine-clearing operations. The system was successfully tested on Maui before the Iwo landing.

Each day, we had to make our way down a winding cliff road from our house to the division's camps and our regular duties. The morning after the big battalion party, I was driving a jeep down the hill with 1st Lt. Joe Dever, the platoon leader I had acquired to replace Bob Reed, when I made him my exec. The left-front tire blew on a curve and the jeep rolled over. I ended up pinned underneath it. I had a crushed left hip, a concussion, and was otherwise pretty beaten up. Some help soon arrived, and they took me to the Kula Sanitarium. I came to on a gurney, looking at a nurse I had partied with the night before as she wiped the blood off my face. I had no idea where I was or what had happened, so I reached up and planted a big kiss on her. That did not go over too well with the head nurse, who shouted, "Get that damn marine outta here!"

The army sent an ambulance for me and transferred me to the 8th Station Hospital down below. I stayed there in a cast through all of December. Of course, I received great treatment. I also had a lot of friends visit, but the real surprise came in the form of General Cates. He came to the hospital with a couple of USO starlets who had come to Maui on a morale tour. Perhaps he thought I needed some female attention to cheer me up. He then pinned the Navy Cross on me while his aide read the citation. It was for the action on Saipan where we assaulted the Japanese lines and I had to change tanks twice. After that, the nurses gave me even more special attention.

The doctors discharged me on New Year's Day, 1945, and I was taken by jeep to the beach and embarked for Iwo Jima. The docs warned me that in about fifteen years I might experience back problems from this injury. My left leg ended up about a third of an inch shorter than the right one, and over the years, with my tennis and running regimen, it wore badly. At that time, however, I was not worried about the future. My company and I were headed for what we knew was going to be a bloody fight.

CHAPTER 8

Infernal Iwo

o sooner was I released from the hospital, than I found myself on board LSM-216, the 4th Marine Division having embarked for another combat mission. After spending all of December in a cast, I found a strange freedom aboard ship. We opened our sealed orders at sea and learned that our next assault was Iwo Jima, one of the Volcano Islands, barely seven hundred miles south of Tokyo! Iwo was too close to the Japanese homeland for this to be an easy job. We knew little then of the pounding the 1st Marine Division had already endured on Peleliu, which meant we knew little yet of the Japanese army's defensive doctrinal changes. No longer would we fight the Japanese in open combat. Now we would have to ferret them out from their carefully concealed and cleverly sited battle positions.

I never liked the thinking behind the design and use of the Landing Ship, Medium (LSM), then being mass-produced for the navy. With a maximum load of six Sherman tanks, it forced a four-way split of my company, whereas the good old LSD carried the entire company on board and allowed each tank to go in on its own dedicated landing craft. In the LSM, I found myself cut off from two of my platoon leaders and Bob Reed as well. Any last-minute changes to the landing plan would require me to give new orders by radio between the ships, instead of the usual face-to-face brainstorming and orders session. Then there was the obvious problem of the LSM being too big a target going to the beach, compared to the little LCMs with their single tanks. The loss of one of these ships meant the loss of one-third of my company's tanks. It was a case of "too many eggs in one basket," as the saying goes.

We had once again been issued a complete set of new tanks for the operation, this time turning in our trusty, twin-diesel-powered M4A2s for the new M4A3 model with its single powerful Ford gasoline engine. It also came with a factory-installed tank-infantry telephone mounted in a metal box on the right-rear fender. Aside from those, we applied all of our usual modifications to the new tanks before embarking. We also added a wrap of spare track blocks to the turret side armor. As a final touch, we mounted domes of heavy wire mesh that rose two inches over the hatches on the turret and hull front. We called these our "birdcages." They were there to prevent enemy infantrymen from placing satchel charges directly on top of those vulnerable points in our armor. It was all well and good that we did these things, because the character of the war was already changing from what we had encountered before. The other company commanders did not employ many of these ideas we developed: the sandbags, the concrete, or the birdcages. I recall being on a hill on Tinian, and about two hundred yards away was a platoon from another company by the edge of a wood. Suddenly a bunch of enemy infantry jumped a tank with a suicide rush. One of the men laid a satchel charge on the commander's hatch, covering it with his body, and knocked out the tank and crew, killing the commander and wounding the men inside. A birdcage would have saved them.

We at first protested the loss of the diesel-powered tanks, because we thought they were less likely to catch fire, and we liked being able to continue operating on a single engine if one was knocked out. In the end, however, I have to admit that the problems the new Japanese defenses posed for us far exceeded the question of what type of fuel or engine we used. Nevertheless, we did miss the superior torque of the twin diesels, which could generate more power and pull us through bogs and sand better than any other engine.

We took the flail tank to Iwo and assigned it to the 2d Platoon. It was the only diesel tank we still had. Hank Bellmon thus had the flail tank and his five tanks on one LSM; Joe Dever's 1st Platoon had five plus me in "Ill Wind," on another; and G. M. English had his five 3d Platoon tanks and the tank retriever on the last one.[1] We made the trip all the way to Iwo on the three LSMs, plus a fourth one carrying the wheeled vehicles and the rest of my company headquarters. Each platoon had

This frontal view of one of our M4A3 medium tanks shows well some of the protective modifications we made. Note the "birdcages" on the hatches and the extra track blocks welded to the front slope.

one of the new flame tanks and four gun tanks. The flame Sherman had been developed in Hawaii by a combined army, navy, and Marine Corps team. They had removed the 75-mm gun and installed a flame weapon, using a worn 75-mm barrel connected by various valves and tubes to a large fuel tank and compressed air cylinders. The compressed air threw out a stream of brown napalm about three-quarters of an inch in diameter. The gunner would walk it onto the target. Once on target, he pressed another switch that ignited the napalm and a stream of fire bathed the target. Its range was over a hundred yards. This tank was one of our best answers to our problems dealing with Japanese fortifications, which became increasingly tough as we progressed across the Pacific.

Our sense of impending trouble did not improve when we stopped at Saipan for the final rendezvous of the assault groups and received the latest intelligence information and photos. We knew that the beaches consisted of volcanic ash extending up to the edge of Airfield No. 1, our initial objective for the assault, but there was no information available regarding its consistency or its depth. We could see hundreds of bomb craters left by the shuttle bombing done by the army air forces and navy, as well as some earlier ship bombardments. We could not gauge the size of these craters, though, and wondered if they would be obstacles for the tanks or not. There certainly were far too many of them to cross if they turned out to be obstacles. Then, at the last minute, came some submarine periscope photos that showed us some of the elevation of the terrain that we could not see in the overhead aerial photography. We were able to identify two terraces fronting the beach, but again we had no idea of the scale of the views. That made it impossible to gauge the height of the terraces, each about twenty yards or more wide, so we could not determine whether or not they would be obstacles. A lot of unknowns faced us as we left Saipan for Iwo, not the least of which was the enemy.

My first concern was getting our tanks ashore and into action. The volcanic ash worried me most. Would tanks be able to plow through the ash, or would we bog down? When I briefed the men on the operation, I emphasized that this was going to be the greatest obstacle. Anyone who found a pathway through the ash would take the lead and the rest of us would follow.

To my last day, I will always remember D-Day on Iwo more clearly than any other day of my life. It was not only the intensity of the enemy fire we all had to endure, but also the fact that my emotions ran the gamut from the excitement of the landing to the most profound frustration I ever experienced in my life, to a sense of relief culminating in a final stage of exhilaration and satisfaction. But I am already ahead of myself.

As in the other landings, I sent my trusty reconnaissance teams in with the first waves of infantry. They would determine at once whether we would bog down and report the same to me immediately via radio. If the answer was that we could bog down there, they were instructed to spread out, one team to the right and the other to the left and find someplace where we could land without bogging down and then report the same to me. C Company would land in the center of the 23d Marines' sector, right on the boundary of the two assaulting battalions, ready to support either or both as necessary. The LSMs remained at some distance as the assault waves of amtracs and landing craft went by. We would go in after the third wave, but before the fourth. The island rumbled with the sound of navy shells and bombs

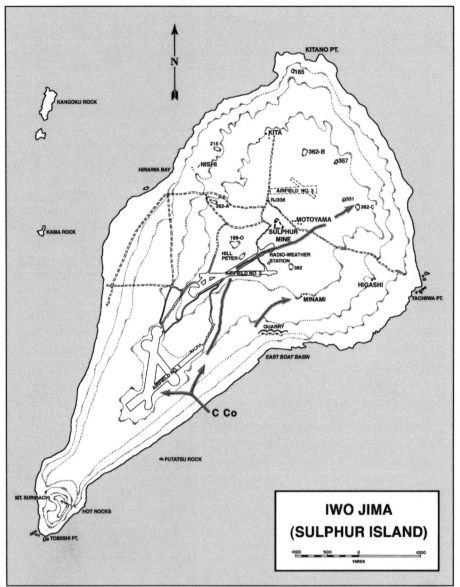

Original USMC map, modified by Charles B. Ash and W. Stephen Hill

falling, but the Japanese did not return much fire. They were saving their effort, maintaining their cover and concealment until the situation became clearer, or so it seemed.

What about my reconnaissance corporals? Shortly after the first wave went in, I received a short, hurried message from one of them on my radio net: "For crissakes don't try to land here, you'll bog down! Wait for us to tell you where." That was not what I had wanted to hear, for it confirmed my worst fears that the sand, ash, terraces, and craters were going to stall us before we could even get off the beach. Nothing more came over the circuit. The fifth wave passed us by. The battalions were calling for tank support. Bob Reed, stationed as usual with the regimental command group, called to say that we were needed ashore. "You've got to go in!" he shouted. I already knew that, of course, I just was hoping for more information.

I decided to make my move. I radioed the other two platoon leaders to watch my LSM and wait and see how we made out. I had no idea how green the skipper and crew of the LSM were.[2] Later, I read that the first LSMs working in the Pacific had been sent on to the Seventh Fleet and the Philippines campaign, leaving us the new arrivals for the Iwo operation. Anyway, after I explained to the skipper, Lt. Chuck Haber, how we wanted to make a gentle, nudging contact with the beach, so we could retract if necessary and try again at another spot, we headed for the near shore. Of course, we wound up going in too fast and hit the beach hard. It seemed as though every gun the Japanese had opened up on us, the first large vessel coming in. They certainly must have suspected that this was the real landing attempt at last. Fortunately, most of their shells and bullets passed through the thin hull without exploding, and none of the holes appeared below the waterline. Haber's after-action report (see appendix 2) certainly shows how hot it was at the time of our beaching, and what the landing craft crews had to endure long after we had disembarked.

I took Ill Wind down the ramp, touched down on the beach, and we bogged down almost immediately. What a fix! Gunnery Sergeant Johnston and I dismounted and dug around the tracks while Cpl. C. B. Ash drove forward and back, but we could not get free. This was getting very frustrating, but some action had to be taken. I radioed Bob Reed that the beach was useless, that we would back off and try again, although I sensed that the ship was already hard aground. We locked up Ill Wind after taking the breechblock out of the 75-mm gun, and reboarded LSM-216. As it turned out, the ship was sufficiently lightened with one less tank that the skipper, Lt. Charles Haber, managed to back off the beach. During this time frame—no more than ten minutes could have elapsed—several wounded marines had reached the ship and boarded on their own. The captain, quite correctly I might add, decided to take them to the nearest hospital LST before resuming our assault mission. By then my sense of frustration had exceeded all known bounds. I really had no idea how to get ashore in such a way that our tanks could maneuver off the beach and come to the aid of the infantry, who were clearly getting the brunt of the fire now, and perform our mission.

What to do now, and where? These two primary thoughts preyed upon me as we neared the LST and transferred our precious cargo of wounded, before turning back toward the beach. This time the skipper picked a spot and eased closer, mindful of the risk of getting the ship stuck, all under unrelenting fire from the Japanese. Gunnery Sergeant Johnston and I stepped off and found the sand and ash to be just as deadly as what we had encountered before. This was really a low point. I had reached the deepest depths of despair and frustration. Suddenly, out of the din and smoke, appeared Cpl. Charles B. Jewell, a driver and one of the recon NCOs who had gone ashore with their walkie-talkies. "I've got a spot!" he shouted above the din, accompanied by a swirl of words describing what he had done and where. All of a sudden, my spirits soared.

We reboarded the ship and had the skipper back off and turn toward the spot Jewell was indicating. I called the other two platoon leaders and told them to have their LSMs follow us. When we landed, the sand held firm, just as Jewell had promised. Moreover, the naval gunfire had torn up the terraces at each level. All we had to do was line up and zigzag over the two collapsed spots and all of a sudden the entire company was out on flat terrain with Corporal Jewell still leading on foot. I was now riding in "Cyclops," having kicked the tank commander down into the gunner's seat for a while. We never did return Ill Wind to action.

We skirted the bomb craters and continued across the waist of the island. The smoke and noise prevented me from seeing much more than Jewell, but then we came upon infantry hugging the deck, which told me that the enemy lay just ahead. I sent Jewell back. Looking forward though my periscope and vision blocks, I could make out seven or eight pillboxes on a line roughly blocking our direction of advance. Now we could go to work! The platoons swung by me and began to work over the pillboxes with their 75-mm cannon and machine guns. The new flame tanks closed the distance and I was immediately impressed with their effect. I later found out that Corporal Schutt, the company photographer and a loader in one of the gun tanks, managed to get some brilliant shots of one of the flame tanks. He used an improvised rig that I had permitted him to mount on his periscope. Although most of Schutt's footage ended up being of the ground and sky, given the way most tanks careen about the land, he captured a flame tank's attack on one pillbox with a few seconds of graphic footage. This clip later found its way into the "V for Victory" documentary on the Iwo and Okinawa operations.[3]

We destroyed all the pillboxes and proceeded uphill with the infantry following us to the airfield. An embankment separated the approach slope from the level plain of the airfield, and after a quick look up on the flat, I reformed the company behind this embankment in order to rearm and count noses. The defilade position offered us some cover from the direct fire whizzing around the island. The infantry stopped and dug in on the edge of the airfield, so we had a relatively secure position at that point.

D-Day on Iwo was the most vivid day of combat I experienced. After the hours of frustration getting ashore, I then felt the greatest exhilaration as we destroyed the bunker line and drove on to Airfield No. 1 by the end of the day, right on schedule. Corporal Jewell later received one of the several Silver Stars I recommended for my men on the island.

One of our flamethrower tanks is shown here in action on Iwo. We borrowed these converted M4-series Sherman tanks from the army. They were originally intended for use on Okinawa, and the Marine Corps did not receive its own until after the Japanese surrendered.

I found out later that the reason I had heard no more messages from him was that his walkie-talkie had literally been shot out of his hands.

I remember the flail tank bogging down. We never did use it. But Sgt. Rick Haddix, the tank commander, told me recently that was not so. He said they got all the way up to the first airfield. There they ran into some flags. They thought they marked a minefield, but it turned out they were a range-finding tool for Japanese heavy mortars. An enemy observation post called fire down on them, and the heavy shells damaged the flail, which they had to evacuate and abandon. It never did have a chance to prove itself. You really need more than one. We might have made more of them if we had gone on and invaded Japan. Haddix later lost a leg to one of their antitank guns while gunning for Hank Bellmon.

■   ■   ■

Our first night ashore proved to be a difficult one. The enemy's heavy artillery fire really gave us no rest. The Japanese fired all calibers of weapons and really did not need to target anything specifically. The two divisions crowded into the narrowest part of the island presented a perfect area target. We were particularly worried about the large spigot mortars and the "screaming meemie" rocket projectiles. In the end, however, these proved far less deadly than the constant rain of mortar bombs and light artillery shells, which the Japanese seemed to have in unlimited supply. Then our ammo dump went up. Resting in the hole we had dug under my tank, I thought it was some of my tanks blowing up and imagined all kinds of catastrophes happening. Surely we had arrived in hell.

The next morning, before dawn, a runner arrived to guide me to the 23d RCT's CP, where Col. Walter W. Wensinger was conducting a briefing for that day's attack. The colonel called for our tanks to lead across the airfield, which seemed the best approach to me as well. However, this was not to be a repetition of my happy ride across the airfield on Roi at all. I led the company over the embankment to a point where we could spread out into our usual V formation, with me at the center. As we moved in column through the infantry, I watched in silent horror as a mortar round landed next to an infantry company commander, a friend of mine through all the 4th Marine Division's battles. He went down, riddled with fragments; killed instantly by the burst. On we went. After forming up, we started across the airfield, buttoned up and ready for action.

Mines! We had run into them before, but never like this. The third tank to my right blew up with a tremendous flash and cloud of dust. I saw the turret fly through the air, led by the flying figure of Gy.Sgt. Joe Bruno, the platoon sergeant of my 1st Platoon. We had run into bombs and torpedo warheads emplaced as land mines. No tank could resist them, and several were completely shattered by them. I know I lost at least three other tanks destroyed, including that of Sgt. Carl D. Smith, perhaps the best of my tank commanders. Cool under fire, he had always moved his tank well, showing great tactical sense.

After crossing the airfield, our tanks withdrew to the start line and we again bivouacked behind the embankment. The infantry held a thin line on the far side, but Airfield No. 1 remained a no-man's land. We found and evacuated Joe Bruno, who had miraculously survived his "flight." Later, we discovered Bruno's gunner, still in the separated turret. It had landed upright, crushing his leg and trapping him inside. Several times during the day, one of the platoon's tanks would pull up near the turret and a crewman would go out the escape hatch in the belly and crawl over to the turret to give him a shot of morphine. The platoon leader, Joe Dever, came to me as we were settling in for the night and asked for permission to lead a rescue patrol after dark. I agreed to this, but cautioned him that I did not want any more casualties.

Dever was a fine officer—big, square, and tough. He had boxed at Princeton, and was one of the few nondrinkers and nonsmokers in our outfit. As he led the battalion surgeon and a corpsman with his little patrol across the barren airfield, they would freeze whenever an illumination flare burst overhead. When they reached the turret of Bruno's tank the corpsman crawled inside and discovered that he could not free the man's shattered leg pinned under the edge of the turret. They would have to amputate it to get him out. The doctor was too fat to crawl inside the turret to perform the operation, so he remained outside. After the corpsman gave the gunner some more morphine, the doctor talked to the corpsman through the pistol port, guiding him through the procedure. Meanwhile, the Japanese had spotted the activity and they fired mortars at the group as it came out. The men were peppered with fragments, and Joe Dever and the doctor had to be evacuated to the beach with the gunner. From there they were taken out to hospital ships.

After the battle was over, I wrote up Silver Star citations for Joe, the corpsman, and the doctor. The gunner was evacuated to a different

**Sergeant Joe Bruno and his gunner survived this encounter
with a large aerial bomb employed as a land mine on Airfield
No. I at Iwo. Three other crewmen were not so fortunate.**

medical facility. He recovered and was eventually discharged medically, but nobody ever had a chance to tell him what had happened. Later, after the war, he heard the story of how Joe Dever saved him. Joe was a successful newspaperman by then. He wrote the "Cholly Knicker-bocker" columns for the Hearst organization. They had a nice reunion in New York many years ago and Joe told me later how moving it was.

The gunner had by that time entered divinity school. I am not surprised at what must be the strength of his beliefs after such a miraculous rescue. He went on to become an ordained minister, raised a family, and sent all his children to college.

■ ■ ■

Our rear echelon personnel—the company headquarters with all the maintenance people (except the retriever crew), cooks, clerks, communicators, and so forth—came ashore on the afternoon of D-plus-2 with my company first sergeant, Russell W. Lippert, in charge. Lippert told me they could see the tanks from the ship. He noticed that we returned to the same spot each night, about two thousand yards from the beach behind the embankment, so he knew right where to join up with us. I was very glad to see Lippert trudging up the hill with all of our headquarters people. We needed somebody to help out with the company administration. Up to that point, the company gunnery sergeant, Sam Johnston, had been submitting all the reports and handling the personnel administration, communications, and other important support tasks without any assistance. First Sergeant Lippert was very capable, and he took charge of all those things and more. The company was really functioning now. We eventually received our two company trucks, which we had fitted with screens and field stoves as mobile kitchens. After that, Steve Pekar, the chief cook, and his gang served hot meals whenever we made it back to the haven behind the berm.

A few hours after Lippert arrived, the field phone buzzed. The caller informed me that division had learned of an attack on the infantry's thinned lines at the north end of the airfield. He told me to watch out for a breakthrough and be prepared to stop it. I called the men to their tanks, and we stood ready, loaded, and briefed. There was a slight hill on the edge of the runway ahead of the embankment, and Lippert and I walked up to it together. I gave him my field glasses and walkie-talkie and told him to keep me informed of what he could see. When I got back to our bivouac site, I sent a couple of men to stay with him.

Division called at about two in the morning and said the attack had been repulsed, so we could stand down. I recalled Lippert and he and the men I sent out to stay with him came sliding back down the embankment. Apparently some Japanese had spotted them coming back, because when he approached me to hand over the glasses and radio, mortar rounds began dropping all around us. At that moment I had what I can best describe as the most eerie feeling of my life: I was standing there in the dark with orange-colored explosions all around, and all of a sudden I felt like I was floating above it in complete silence, watching rounds drop all around us. My gosh, I thought, I'm dead! So this is what it feels like. It really was not so bad, floating there over everything else. "Well," I said to myself, "if this is what it's like to be dead, it's not too bad."

Then reality set in. I realized I was not dead, was not floating, but everything was silent. Our corpsman, Perry Wappes, was looking straight at me and I could see his lips moving but no words came out. I shook my head and said: "Wappes, whatever you're saying I can't hear. I can't hear a thing." He pulled out a flashlight and peered into my ears. When he was down he moved back directly in front of me and slowly mouthed the words, "It's no wonder, your eardrums were blown in," while pointing at his own ears. The shelling had stopped, and we looked around and saw men gathering. Lippert was lying flat on his back. He had a little hole in his chest, and when we turned him over we discovered that half of his back was gone. A couple of other men were dead, and several more had been wounded, including one of my jeep drivers, John L. Cupp. Spencer Toles, the other jeep driver, was not hurt. Cupp's stomach was torn open. Sam Littlepage and another corpsman pulled Cupp under my tank to try to give first aid. The rest of us crawled under the tank, too, for protection. The corpsman pulled out a flashlight and examined Cupp's wounds. He shook his head as he gave him a shot of morphine and tried to cheer Cupp up, saying that he would be down on the beach by first light. It was a "million-dollar wound," he said, and they would put him on a ship and send him home. Cupp did not last more than an hour or so.

A little while later, Bob Reed arrived. They had been told back at the CP that I was dead, and the regimental commander had instructed him to go back, take command, and send a new liaison officer to take his place. Reed had gone through several hundred yards of no-mans' land to reach us. We exchanged notes and decided that I could still run the company by writing orders. He went back, and my hearing began to return by morning. Within a day or so I was back to normal. The corpsman wanted to write me up for a Purple Heart, as he was supposed to do, but after seeing Lippert and Cupp die, I could not take it. I told him not to do it, and I am glad I did not receive the award.

A year or so ago, I learned about a postscript to this event from a *Leatherneck* magazine article by Joe Rosenthal about the two flag raisings he photographed on Iwo. Joe and several other correspondents had gone ashore and he had no helmet. Somebody pointed out a pile of helmets taken from dead marines on the beach and told him to take one. He wrote that he had often wondered about the man whose helmet he had. The name written on it was Lippert.

After the battle, when we were back on Maui, I wrote to the families of my dead marines and told them how their son or husband had died, how heroic and good he had been, and so forth. I wrote to Lippert's wife, telling her what a great man he was and what a loss his death was for all of us. She wrote a scathing reply. She was understandably upset, but she accused me of putting her husband in an untenable position and getting him killed. I had tried to explain what he had done, the great

The company dozer tank was temporarily out of action with mine damage during the Iwo battle. Note the protective modifications to this M4A3 tank: wood and concrete added to the sides, sandbags on the engine deck, extra track blocks on the turret, and "birdcages" covering the hatches. The extra fuel tank was used to carry water for the tank crew and accompanying infantry. My tank driver, Cpl. Charles B. Ash, RIGHT, stands beside the tank with Cpl. Nile E. Darling, a mechanic. I came ashore in this tank after my own bogged down during the first landing attempt.

service that he had rendered, but she took it badly. Hers was the only negative response I got after writing roughly forty such letters during the entire war.

■   ■   ■

Seeing the flag raised on Mount Suribachi had a tremendous positive effect on morale of all us on Iwo and the nearby ships. Suribachi, by far the highest point on the island, was clearly visible to everybody on the ground. From its summit, the Japanese were able to see every move we made. It was a magnificent observation post for directing the gunners up north as well as firing down on us, so that we were trapped between two fires. Both the 3d and 4th Divisions faced north with part of the 5th Division, with Suribachi behind all but the 5th Division troops charged with taking it. When the flag went up, it meant that all of us no longer had to worry about what was at our backs, firing on us. We were no longer caught in the middle. Until that point, the outcome of the battle had seemed in doubt. However, when we saw that flag atop Suribachi, we knew that we were winning and that we would eventually take the island. Marines all over the island rose up and cheered at the sight of that flag going up. It was as if their team had just scored the go-ahead touchdown in the most important football game of their lives. Even those in foxholes stopped, stood up, and cheered.

However, it took several more weeks of hard fighting to secure that terrible island. We encountered our first antitank gun on the island in the vicinity of Airfield No. 2. It was a powerful one. Several tanks dueled with it without knocking it out. We took some hits, and we left it as a draw. At about that time, the division pulled the 23d Marines out of the line and the 21st Marines took its place. The 3d Marine Division at last was coming ashore, but the 21st was the only regiment in thus far, and none of Lt. Col. Holly Evans's 3d Tank Battalion vehicles had landed yet to reinforce it. For the moment, the 21st Marines was attached to our 4th Marine Division, and my company logically reinforced it as the infantrymen of the 23d Marines finally got a short break and filed to the rear.

I was looking forward to seeing and working with Col. Hartnoll J. Withers, the 21st's commander. "Barney" Withers was a pioneer tank officer. He had formed the 1st Tank Company in 1937. It later became the 1st Scout Company, which I had joined in 1941. He subsequently commanded the 2d Tank Battalion upon its formation in late 1941, and he took a lot of his officers and men with him to form the 3d Tank Battalion, 3d Marine Division, in 1942. He stayed with the 3d Division for the rest of the war. When he made colonel, he became the first tanker to command an infantry regiment—something almost unheard of in the modern Marine Corps.

We met in his command post, and I was stunned when he tersely told me that his infantry would lead the way in the morning. My company was to "keep out of the way, we'll call you up if we need you," or words to that effect. I was pretty proud of the job my tankers had done thus far. We had saved the infantry a lot of casualties. Although the 4th Division had been very green when it first arrived at Camp Pendleton, we had acquired a lot of skill and teamwork in tank-infantry tactics. I could not believe that we were expected to sit this one out.

But that is just what we did, at least for a while. The 21st Marines advanced a few hundred yards toward Airfield No. 2 before it was stopped cold by the terrible cross fire the Japanese had formed with their weapons, which were sited in a maze of pillboxes, caves, and firing positions—all backed by an equally well-designed network of antitank guns. Withers finally called for us at midday and we raced forward to give covering fire as they pulled back almost to the start line.

When the 3d Tank Battalion finally came ashore, Rip Collins, who was commanding the 5th Marine Division's 5th Tank Battalion, convinced the corps commander that we ought to mass the tanks of all three divisions in order to overcome the Japanese defenses. I would like to think that Maj. Gen. Harry Schmidt, who had been our division commander on Saipan, believed in the value of tanks because of what we had shown him in the 1944 battles, but I do not know that for a fact. At any rate, Schmidt made Collins the commander of the massed tank units and Rip asked me to function as his executive officer. I was getting nowhere with Barney Withers, who seemed to be trying to emulate the most basic of all infantry officers, so I was glad to lend a hand, leaving Bob Reed capably in charge of C Company for the moment. We planned through the night to bring all the tanks on line for a mass attack across Airfield No. 2. By this time, however, our "mass" was becoming thinner. The 4th Tank Battalion reported only twenty-eight tanks in action, and the 5th Tank Battalion another thirty-four at the end of D-plus-3. Assuming that Holly Evans had all forty-five of his 3d Tank Battalion vehicles up and running, this should have been enough to overwhelm the Japanese defenses.

**C Company tanks in action on Iwo Jima with marine infantry
watching in the foreground.**

Attacking on D-plus-5, we found that the tank battalions could not
carry out the plan. The ground around Airfield No. 2 was much more
broken than was the case with the first airfield we overran. We had to
use narrower routes among the larger rocks and ravines that covered the
middle and northern parts of the island. Here, the Japanese had once
again strewn lots of mines, including some of their supermines. Most
of the tanks were jammed up on these routes for the rest of the morning while the mines were being cleared, then they pushed on to the near
edge of the airfield to support the infantry's advance by fire. In the end,
the airfield did not fall until D-plus-7, after the infantry and tanks had
picked their way across in the face of intense fire from all arms.

Our ability to maneuver in front of the Japanese was already coming
to an end. As V Corps advanced beyond Airfield No. 2, the Motoyama
Plateau and the Japanese main line of resistance on Iwo lay ahead. The
enemy had to be literally dug out of his rocky lair by teams of infantry
companies and small numbers of tanks. We often had to use tank doz-
ers or armored bulldozers to cut a path for the gun and flame tanks to
follow. The flame tanks, nicknamed "Zippos," proved their value here.
They could shoot their flaming rods of napalm into the caves and pillboxes very accurately. We escorted them carefully with gun tanks and
never lost a single one in action.

We had more than a few misunderstandings with the infantry as we poured fire into enemy positions only to pull back when we ran out of ammo. The expressions on the infantrymen's faces were pitiful and they yelled to us to stay. When we explained that we were only going back for more ammunition and would be right back (really an hour or more would be lost), they calmed down.

After the mass tank attack, the 3d Marine Division completed its landing and we said good-bye to the 21st Marines. The 3d Division did a good job in the Motoyama Plateau battle, but we were glad to go back to the 23d Marines and work with people with whom we had trained. It all goes to show you how important it is to know your people, units, and capabilities before the battle. Improvising during the battle can seldom make up for real teamwork among seasoned units.

In contrast to my experience with Barney Withers, I met many other officers who impressed me with their skill and abilities. An army major, Sam Littlepage, stayed with me during most of the fighting to watch the flame tanks in action. He later became the executive officer of the army's 713th Tank Battalion, which provided all the flame tank support on Okinawa—an early example of "jointness." Anyway, Sam was with us every day, every step of the way on Iwo, observing and crewing tanks. He impressed us all with his courage and good humor. By our standards, he became a marine.

We also welcomed 1st Lt. Sonny Franks, a marine Corsair pilot assigned to us to observe air support from the ground. I recognized Sonny because he was one of the few two-year All-American football players in those days coming, in this case, from the University of Minnesota. I saw a lot of Sonny Franks after the war. I told Cpl. Wayland Ashcraft, "If anything happens to this aviator, I'll kill you," so Ashcraft dug holes for him and generally helped keep Sonny alive, even though he was going all around the island looking to see what air support could do for ground troops. After the war, Sonny became a running back for the New York Giants for seven or eight years. When they came to Los Angeles to play the Rams, Reed and I would do the town with him at night. He retired and bought a house on Long Island, after which I lost track of him.

Close air support made a very big impression upon us at Iwo because we had never seen so much of it. Because of the hidden Japanese positions, though, the pilots had to come down very low in order to pinpoint their attacks. We were sitting in our tanks watching a number of these guys roll in on their targets. We chattered jokingly on the radio about each pilot, saying, "That one is married," if he pulled up high, and "That one is single," if he came in low. Then one of the fighter-bombers rolled in and planted his napalm right on top of English's tank! We all ran over with our hand fire extinguishers. We were relieved to see G. M. pop out with his, too. Luckily, nothing was seriously damaged. However, we also learned that some of these weapons were not as effective as they had appeared.

■ ■ ■

Strange things happen in combat almost every day, and your memory becomes blurred. Corporal Bart Corricelli recently wrote about an incident for our USMC tankers' association, after my driver egged him on.

Iwo Jima, 2-3 PM, 27th Feb 1945 give or take a day, in the Co. bivouac area.

Now it can be told—the Truth—the whole Truth and nothing but the truth! The almost killing of 1st LT Robert Reed, XO, C Company 4th Tank Bn.

LT Reed swore—that we—Sgt Jim Parker, tank commander of "Cyuzie", number 36, the XO's tank and Bart Corricelli, Cpl assistant driver, intended to purposely and willfully do away with him.

Let me start at the beginning. It is a sunny and warm day. We had come back from somewhere between Motoyama #1 and #2. Being out most of the morning and part of the afternoon, we grabbed something to eat, had a smoke, and bat the shit for a while. "Smokey" Mills our gunner, Mickey McMahon, loader and Welsh, driver wandered off, after we had reloaded with 75mm shells, 30 cal MG ammo and a cylinder of napalm for our small flame thrower. Sgt Parker decided to clean the 75. I got the ram rod and cleaned the bore and climbed into the turret with Parker. He was on the loaders side and I set down in the gunners seat. We spent 45 minutes taking apart, cleaning and oiling the breech block. We did some final wiping all around the breech.

As were going thru all this cleaning and bullshitting about why we should clean the guns just so we can kill Japs, I said lets kill them with a dirty gun. At this point in time, Lt. Reed is walking by our tank, and within 5 feet of the 75mm muzzle, not knowing that in a second he is going to have the shit scared out him and almost on a one way trip to heaven or where ever. Now back to the turret.

Parker says, "I think I'll slam one in to make sure everything is working." I said "Bullshit, you do that and we'll have to clean it again." But I was out ranked. Parker reached back and pulled up an AP round (armor piecing). There is no ceremonious thing you go through before you do this, like, "ready-here goes!" He just grabbed it and slammed it in the breech. Immediately " WHOOMP". "What the fuck happened Bart." "Shit I don't know"—there's a pause—After looking around—"Jesus, somebody left a helmet wedged on the foot trigger. SEE—now we're going to have to clean this SOB again."

"Dammit, just like I told you!!!" Then, we heard a commotion outside. "What the fuck you guys trying to do in there?" We jump out of the hatches and the first thing I see is a guy laying just about at the end of the 75mm tube covered in volcanic ash. I said, "holy shit, we killed the fucking lieutenant." Jim said, "No we didn't, he's moving." Fortunately for us, Reed is only shaken up. His shirt pocket, with a couple of pens and a pack of cigarettes, was blown off his shirt. His face and body are completely covered in ash and he is not only shaken up, due to the fact it was an AP instead of an HE, which would have killed him instantly, also, if he had been a millisecond sooner, Parker and Corricelli would have, were sure, been court martialed for involuntary manslaughter. Most fortunately for Jim and Bart was the fact that the cannon was depressed as far as it goes and the fired round went into the ground immediately in front of the tank, instead of being elevated and that round tearing into a bunch of our own guys and killing them. This is known as friendly fire. Then we would have been in deep shit, up to our necks, more likely "stretched necks," cause we would have been hung.

Needless to say, Lt. Reed was pissed to the gills and rightfully so. He also promised to hang our asses out to dry. After brushing himself off he stomped down to the company CP and Major Neiman. The calm and cool leadership of the major evidently cooled the hot-tempered, ash-covered LT down, for we didn't hear very much about it after that. Again fortunately, because of the heavy fighting we had going on with the Japs, that we didn't want to give up that god forsaken piece of shit they called an island.

The only mild repercussions we got were from our own troops, like: quote "my grandmother could have stuck in his ear" "you guys better get your eyes checked" "you guys missed getting rid of a pain in the ass for us." unquote.

You can tell by now that LT Reed was not a much loved man, being the "Hard Nosed Ass-Hole" that he was. I guess he tried too hard to be another "Chesty Puller, him being about the same size as "Chesty." All in all, he was a good Marine LT.

And so the saga ended on that fateful day of Feb 27, give or take.

Parker and my self felt a little remorse about scaring the hell out of Lt Reed, but we were doing something to keep ourselves in the position of not having any misfires or having the cannon jam on us,— God forbid!! Because the Japs had a few 47s and we didn't want to be non-combatants in a moving tank. As it turned out it took us 36 days to secure Iwo at the cost of too many good marines. We were fortunate enough to survive.[4]

The island was declared secure on March 26, but small actions continued even after V Corps had left the island. To this day, I remain a little bitter that the 3d Marine Division's third regiment never landed to take up the fight. It was held out as a "floating reserve," and was still afloat when the battle ended. Those of us who fought on Iwo considered this a tragic mistake. We felt that a coordinated attack by a fresh, full-strength regiment of over three thousand marines could have shortened the battle by a week or more and saved many marines' lives. Instead, we fed a few thousand raw replacements into the lines to "fight" along-side marines and NCOs and officers they did not know and who were themselves truly battle weary.

We only had nine tanks left running at the end of the Iwo Jima campaign. In the photo where I am briefing my company, we appear a bit more relaxed because the main fight was over and only some mopping-up actions continued. I do not think all the tanks in the background were running. I was telling my troops what I knew was going on and when we might expect to get off the island, which we all were anxious to do. We had lost too many of our men and seen too much of that awful place. We left the tanks behind this time, for good reason.

■   ■   ■

We received a very touching reception back on Maui. The people had read the press reports about the battle of Iwo Jima, and they knew that the 4th Marine Division was there. When the surviving elements (I really mean "remnants") of the division returned, the whole island turned out to greet us. There were lots of bands, banners, and hula troupes. We saw signs that read, "Welcome home Maui's own" or

**Here I am talking to my company shortly after the Iwo Jima
fighting ended in March, 1945.**

"Maui's Marines—We Love You!" and other similar slogans. We had
returned there after each campaign or battle of "our" Pacific War, only
to be called away again. This time, however, we were there to stay until
our unit disbanded in November, 1945.

While we were en route to Maui, we heard about the Tenth Army's
landing on Okinawa. It was Sunday, April Fools' Day, 1945. Bob Reed
and I were walking topside along the weather deck of the USS
Rockbridge, thinking about how far we had come now that the war was
at the doorstep of the Japanese home islands, when Bob asked me what
I thought we should do after the war. I am convinced that anybody who
was on Iwo for the entire thirty-three days, even if not wounded, walked
off the island a different person. We may not have been suffering from
shell shock, but all of us had to be more serious and contemplative
about life than we were before. No other battle affected me that way.
With that as background, it is easy to understand how we felt.

I remember thinking, those poor bastards landing on Okinawa, it
must be just like Iwo. In the end it was tough, but more spread out in

time and space. We did not know until later that the landing on
Okinawa was virtually unopposed. We talked quietly about it, glad that
we were not involved. Then, out of the blue, Reed said: "Bob, what if
we're both alive and well when the war ends? What are we going to do?"
I looked at him with amazement and said something like: "Well, for
Christ's sake, this war is never going to end! It's just one damn island
after another. We've been lucky so far. What makes you think that our
luck will hold out forever?" Reed said, "Wait a minute. The war *is* going to end, and it's going to end soon. Iwo is only a few hundred miles
from Tokyo, and Okinawa is only a few hundred miles from Japan's
other main islands. We're going to be there pretty soon and the war is
going to end then." I pooh-poohed that, but he was persistent. Finally
I said, "Well, okay, what about it?" Bob stared at me for a moment and
then asked, "Well, are we going to stick together?"

We made three vows that evening. First, if we were indeed both alive
and well at the end of the war, we would stick together—meaning we
would both either stay in the Corps or go inactive together. Second, if
we got out, we would go into business together. Third, if that happened, we would stay as close to Maui as possible, which meant living in Southern California. We did not want to live on Maui because
it was an island and we wanted to live on the mainland, but we figured
that we would be going back as often as possible. As it turned out, I did
not get back to Maui for seventeen years, and Reed stayed away even
longer.

Anyway, that was how we sowed the seeds of our postwar careers
together. The reasons, though, were more poignant. We felt strongly
that ours was the best tank company in the Marine Corps. Over a period of two years we had trained and led it through some of the most
violent battles of the war. We had each saved the other's lives, so we
were truly blood brothers. We had enormous faith and trust in each
other and were aware of each other's strengths and shortcomings. We
learned that each had different abilities that complemented the other.
We had had a trial "marriage," forged in fire, during which we learned
a great deal about running an organization, picking people, and training and motivating them so that they would follow us to hell and back.
We believed that with that kind of background we would be able to
build a successful civilian company and make some money. But we
loved the Marine Corps and Marine Corps life, except for getting shot

at, so we would have to make a very important decision later to stay in or get out. Nonetheless, we resolved that night that whatever we did, we would do it together.

I remember that April Fools' Day conversation like it was yesterday, and to this day I cannot believe how introspective we had become after that terrible battle. It truly cast our destiny.

CHAPTER 9
Okinawa
The Last Battle

D ick Schmidt had asked me more than once to be his battalion executive officer, as I was the senior major of the four we had in the battalion. Leo Case, for example, had been in the second officer candidate class. But I just could not be Dick's exec. He was a good friend, but I recognized that he was not a great commanding officer and that I was better off running my own company. Besides, I wanted to command a battalion of my own. After Iwo, we learned that Schmidt was leaving for another assignment, as he made the rounds in the bivouac area, saying good-bye. He was getting a staff job at the Fleet Marine Force–Pacific headquarters in Hawaii and I, being senior to the rest of the officers of the battalion, was going to be his replacement. I thought that was great, and immediately began thinking about how I would change things, welding the three separate companies into a real battalion command. I took over as the acting battalion commander three or four days after we got back from Maui, and Reed, by then a captain, was given command of C Company.

General Cates called me to his headquarters and told me he was happy that I was commanding the 4th Tank Battalion and that he expected great things of me. After receiving that blessing, I started working on the organization that I wanted to create. The reason I was so enthusiastic about taking command of the battalion after Iwo was that I was convinced it had not been run the way it should. Having been a major and company commander for two years, I was confident that I could handle the job.

Much to my surprise, however, Lt. Col. Harvey "Wally" Walseth arrived in a jeep a couple of days later. I had last seen Wally when he was a company commander, and I thought he was a real nice guy. He had commanded A Company, 1st Tank Battalion, on Guadalcanal and served as General Vandergrift's senior tank officer on the island. After the 1st Marine Division left Guadalcanal, he returned to the States and was assigned to the Headquarters, Marine Corps (HQMC) staff. At first I thought he was a visitor from the division staff, but then I saw a seabag in the back of the jeep and wondered what he was doing here.

After we greeted each other warmly, he said: "I was in Washington for two years, and I was supposed to go back overseas. I guess somebody looked and saw that there was a tank lieutenant colonel going to the Pacific and there was a tank battalion without one, so here I am. I'd like you to be my exec." I was madder than hell! I had declined the same offer from Schmidt, but what could I do? I had been the acting CO and then lost the battalion in just a few days. I figured my only other option was going to a staff job somewhere, and I surely did not want that, so I became the executive officer and we got along just fine. When I told him what I had intended to do with the battalion, he immediately agreed. We continued to implement the plan I had developed.

A week or so later, Walseth called all four of us majors together and showed us a message from HQMC ordering the battalion to furnish a major to the 1st Marine Division on Okinawa to take command of the 1st Tank Battalion. Apparently Lt. Col. Jeb Stuart had become a casualty. Wally said he thought it was unfair. He said he was sure none of us wanted to go to Okinawa so soon after coming off of Iwo, but somebody was needed. He suggested that we draw straws to see who would go. While he was talking I had been thinking: My God! I can get out of this situation and get a battalion in combat. That was exactly what I had wanted all along. "You won't have to do that, colonel," I said. "I volunteer. I want to go." The other three majors were delighted, but he was clearly a little puzzled. "It's nothing to do with you Wally," I told him later, when we were alone. "I really would like to have a battalion of my own, and this is my chance." I really meant it.

The orders said I was to go to Okinawa as soon as possible, so I had only a few days left on Maui. There was an institution on the island known as the Puunene Athletic Club, run by the big sugar company at Puunene. It consisted of a very nice dining room, snack bar, a fine swimming pool, and three tennis courts. My company officers and I had been made honorary members of the club because we trained nearby at the end of a long, winding macadam road, splendidly isolated from the rest of the division. The companies' tanks were grouped in separate parks so as to keep them off the roads. The troops were trucked in and back for meals and work details each day. At about 4 P.M. we sent everyone back with one officer and the rest of us would go to the club to swim, drink, and relax.

We got to know a middle-aged Japanese lady who ran the dining room and the snack bar. We all called her "Mom." She had three or four seventeen- or eighteen-year-old Japanese girls who waited on the tables. The night before I left the island for Okinawa, the battalion officers threw a party for me, and she set out a cake as big as a desktop with a Marine Corps emblem and the words "Good Luck Major, Aloha," which I thought was very nice. The next morning I flew to Pearl Harbor in a Marine Corps plane and spent a day there before flying to Guam. While I was on Oahu I went up to the hospital at Aiea to see Joe Dever. He was still in bad shape from the wounds he had received on Iwo, but we had a great reunion, and Joe showed me his usual good spirits.

My plane took off in the late afternoon for the long flight to Guam, with a refueling stop at Kwajalein. It was a four-engine plane, a brand-new DC-4 assigned to an admiral as his personal aircraft. He rode in a forward compartment all to himself, and three colonels or lieutenant colonels and one major—me—were flying as passengers. The plane was magnificent: the walls were paneled and the main cabin had two tables with green felt tops and four club chairs per table. There was nothing else in the compartment. Directly behind the main cabin was a compartment with four bunk beds. Behind that was a head, and behind that was a galley and crew compartment for the stewards, the plane captain, and so forth. After we took off, one of the stewards informed us that they would be serving dinner at six o'clock and asked how would we like our steaks.

That was really some flight! We four passengers sat around talking and having a great time. The stewards set the other table with a white tablecloth, glasses, and tableware, and said dinner would be served in five minutes. They cleared the table after we ate, and we played cards until around nine, when a steward appeared and told us we would land on Guam the next day. He said if we wanted to sleep, they had turned down our beds. It was like a very fine hotel. I slept very comfortably, waking briefly during the refueling stop at Kwajalein. At 5:15 A.M., the steward shook me awake and asked me how I would like my eggs for breakfast. He added that we would be landing on Guam in forty-five minutes. I have never since had a flight like that!

It was raining like hell when we landed on Guam. I had a friend there, Capt. Larry Snowden, who later became chief of staff of the Marine Corps. He had been a rifle company commander in the 23d Marines and we saw a lot of combat and worked well together. He went to 3d Marine Division after Saipan and Tinian, and he was in Iwo as a 3d Division Company Commander. I was able to get word to him before I left that I was coming through. As it turned out, the control tower advised us that there would be no flights to Okinawa for at least another day because of bad weather, and they would advise us when they had scheduled a flight. Larry invited me to share his tent, and gave his telephone number to the control shack. I spent the next three days there because of the backlog of flights. We saw a few navy nurses he had met and had a nice time on the beach.

■   ■   ■

The next plane was a DC-4 like the admiral's, but it proved to be very different inside. The cabin was lined with canvas seats on the sides, and a pile of mail sacks and boxes was strapped down on the floor. There were not enough seats, so I just curled up on the floor with the bags. It was cold, but things got hotter when we got to Okinawa. The Japanese had just launched their ill-fated air assault (the one-way trip of the battleship *Yamato* was part of it) and everybody was trigger happy. The pilot told us we would be landing soon and then, bingo, we started to take evasive action. Things flew around inside and you could see puffs of antiaircraft fire through the window ports! The gunners thought we were Japanese, so they let us have it. Fortunately, it only lasted for a minute and we were not hit. We looked out on the airfield and saw burning aircraft and the bodies of dead Japanese troops lying nearby. I had missed the amphibious landing, which was mostly unopposed, only to be almost shot down coming in by air!

I had no idea where anything was on the island, so I checked in at the control shack. "I'm supposed to go to the 1st Tank Battalion, 1st Marine Division," I said. "Do you have any idea where they are or how to get there?" The duty clerk said, "Well they came through here a couple of days ago." The battle of Naha had just taken place, and the 6th Marine Division was on the extreme right of the front line on the west coast of the island, with the 1st Marine Division next to it and the rest of the army divisions continuing in line across the island. I asked the guy if he had any idea how to get to the division. He pointed to a road a couple of hundred yards away that was choked with traffic, and said, "Just go over there and get on one of those vehicles headed south."

I thanked the man and walked over to the road. A few minutes later, a truck driver offered to take me to the 1st Division's headquarters. We went through Naha and there were just three things left standing: a two-story stone building with a little tower, a lone palm tree, and some concrete poles for the streetcar lines, but with no wires of course. Everything else was just gone. I had never seen a city so flattened.

We eventually came to the 1st Marine Division headquarters. I found the division sergeant major and he called the 1st Tank Battalion sergeant major, who immediately dispatched a jeep for me. The first guy to greet me was Jeb Stuart. I could not believe it. We had a great reunion. I was delighted to see him alive and well, but his being there meant I had again been thwarted in my quest for a battalion command.

I first met Jeb at New River when I was with the 1st Tank Battalion and he was visiting us on orders of HQMC. We recognized him as a first rate officer right from the start. I later got to know Jeb well at Jacque's Farm, which he visited several times during my tour there. I learned later that he had become the executive officer of the 1st Corps Tank Battalion after returning from the tank officer course at Fort Knox, where he had been graded a superior student—which was not surprising to us, of course. We even went to Tijuana together once. It did not take much time to become friends in wartime. I had a very high regard for him and was glad that he was okay. I told him why I was there, and he said he had known that I was coming but he never could figure out why. When I told him we had been informed he was a casualty, he said, "Well, I do have amoebic dysentery, and while it may be a pain in the ass literally and figuratively, I'm not leaving this battalion until the battle's over. If you want it then, you can have it. Meanwhile, you'll take over as my exec." There were no other majors, so Capt. Dick Munger, a fine officer who had been serving as his exec, became the battalion operations officer.

After I retired and Suzy and I moved to the California desert, we were visiting with neighbors who said they had a close friend named Dick

Munger who had been a World War II marine tank officer. They said he came from Spokane (they were snowbirds) and had bought a place nearby. When they asked if I had known him, I told them about our previous relationship, and we all laughed. Talk about Marine Corps tankers living in a small world! Dick was a terrific guy who looked just like one of my favorite movie actors, Spencer Tracy. We saw a lot of him, but he developed a cancer a few years ago and died shortly thereafter.

■　■　■

I joined the battalion after the Sugar Loaf battle and before Kunishi Ridge. Shortly after my arrival Jeb said: "Bob, you have more combat experience in tanks than anyone else in the Marine Corps, and what I'd like you to do as my exec is be my eyes and ears. I can't be everywhere, and I need to know as much as possible." After that, whenever we were engaged I would go out by jeep or on foot and observe the platoons supporting the infantry, consider whether we should do it that way, and come back and report to Jeb. We would then talk it over and decide what to do.

Jeb had come up with a tactical procedure he called "processing" that he used to support the infantry when they encountered Japanese defenses dug into one ridgeline after another. We would send out anywhere from a platoon to a company of tanks as much as eight hundred yards beyond our lines. Infantry fire teams would follow the tanks and protect them from close assaults by concealed Japanese. A section or platoon, depending on the size of the element we sent out, would go far forward and draw fire, if necessary. Then they and the rest of the platoon or company would then fire 75-mm high-explosive rounds at every possible cave or emplacement on the Japanese-held ridgeline. They employed both quick acting and delayed fuses, and usually threw in some white phosphorous as well.

Any Japanese antitank gun that opened up got immediate attention from the overwatching tanks and was quickly smothered with fire. The tanks would fire out to the limits of their observation, usually about fifteen hundred yards. That done, the infantry would then come forward and move past the tanks onto the ridgeline as far as we could provide direct fire. Then we would send the tanks up to join them and repeat the procedure.

Sometimes additional tanks would come out to replace platoons sent back to rearm. Jeb had begun using this procedure on Peleliu, and it worked very well on Okinawa. According to his after-action report, we did not lose a single tank to infantry close assault, which was a big improvement over earlier Marine Corps battles. Antitank guns and mines caused most of our casualties. I saw four different ridgelines taken this way, but in the last effort to take Kunishi Ridge, the last line of Japanese resistance in the south, we had some problems.

Most Japanese antitank weapons had only a marginal effect on our M4 medium tanks, which was one of the reasons we abandoned the light tank in Marine Corps service. At first, marine tankers encountered few Japanese antitank guns, and those were only the 37-mm variety, which was standard in most armies at the beginning of the war. However, as the Pacific War developed and the Japanese recognized the power of our tanks, they began to emplace 47-mm antitank guns on their islands. They developed that gun in 1941, and at close range it could penetrate the side armor of the M4 Sherman, whereas the 37-mm gun could not. When our intelligence people told us about it, we added concrete to our wooden side protection to resist those guns. Of course, we never knew when another gun might be introduced, and an older 75-mm antiaircraft gun almost proved to be our undoing. I am glad to say that we never ran into one in my C Company, but it probably was the gun we ran into on Fathers' Day, June 17, 1945 on Okinawa.[1]

Both Jeb and I were watching the action that day. There remains a lot of debate about what kind of gun it was. Bob Boardman calls it a 76-mm gun in his personal account, but some of us thought it was at least as big as a German 88-mm gun.[2] Whatever it was, it knocked the hell out of our tanks. We were ready to start processing, and we sent 2d Lt. Gerry Adkinson's platoon over the ridge we occupied. Then *bang-bang*, two of the tanks were blown up. Adkinson was knocked out of his tank and Boardman, his driver, had come out, too. We all thought Adkinson was a goner, but we thought that Boardman was alive, so we sent some guys down there in a tank to crawl out and get them. Sniper fire was hitting all over, and the gunner in that tank thought it was coming from where Adkinson was lying, so he opened up. By God, he shot Adkinson in the hand! Gerry was wearing a pair of red socks his wife had sent him, and when this gunner shot him, he raised his leg up in the air. We saw those red socks and somebody shouted, "He's alive!" Several guys rushed down there despite the rifle fire and dragged him back. He survived and made a complete recovery. He was still on active duty in 1952 at Camp Pendleton, and while I was visiting G. M. English there, Adkinson took my wife Suzy for a tank ride.

Anyway, I told Jeb that this would be a good time to use air spotting to get that gun. I told him about our experience on Tinian using the OY-type observation aircraft for spotting.[3] He called division and they immediately tasked the OY squadron. I went over to tell them what we wanted, intending to be the guy who went up with a radio and smoke grenades to spot the gun. When I arrived at our assigned OY's location I received a message from Jeb saying that he was sending the battalion S2 (intelligence officer) to go up and that I was not to go. When the OY was airborne and on station, we repeated the processing drill, and the enemy gun opened fire. The S2 saw it and threw a couple of smoke grenades from the plane. The tanks started firing at the smoke and he directed their fire over the radio. After a little of this they managed to silence the gun. Meanwhile, ground fire hit the plane and a round went through our lieutenant's knee. The doctors wound up having to amputate his leg.

Two 7th Marines companies infiltrated to the top of Kunishi Ridge that night, but the Japanese rallied so strongly that no infantry units were able to cover the ground the next day to reinforce them or bring up supplies. They suffered a lot of wounded as the day went on, and it looked like they were going to be cut off and overwhelmed. We decided to try sending our tanks up to their position with supplies and replacements and then return with their casualties. We took three men out of each tank, leaving the driver and tank commander, and loaded three or four infantrymen as well as ammo and other supplies, including replacement weapons, aboard each vehicle. We made three runs that day, depositing fifty-four replacements and bringing out numerous casualties. We used the belly escape hatch to unload men and supplies and then load the wounded aboard.

The remainder of the two battalions made it to the ridge the next night, but the enemy remained underground and directed mortar and artillery fire into the position. We continued our daily runs to sustain the ridge enclave and a similar foothold in the 1st Marines' sector at a cost of twenty-two vehicles knocked out or damaged. During that week of operations, our tanks carried some 550 troops forward, along with ninety tons of ammunition, replacement weapons, medical supplies, rations, water, and wire. They returned with more than six hundred casualties. I do not think anything like that has been attempted since.

■ ■ ■

Kunishi Ridge was the final Japanese line of resistance. The 1st Tank Battalion never went forward of that line. A couple of days later, the 8th

Marines, reinforced, landed and joined the division. Captain Ed Bale commanded their attached tank company—A Company, 2d Tank Battalion—and he came over to report to Jeb. We told him all we could about the conditions we had faced. As they deployed for the attack the next morning, Jeb—who was totally fearless—wanted to go up with them. "C'mon, Bob, let's go see what's going on," he said. No Jeb, let's not! I thought. Of course I went anyway, Jeb dragging me along as a less-than-willing accomplice.

I will never forget it. A rock outcropping extended beyond and above a ravine that went down several hundred feet. The marine lines ended at the ravine, but the outcropping went out another couple of hundred yards. "Let's go out there and watch this dogfight," said Jeb. So we crawled out there, all alone in Jap territory, and lay on that finger of terrain with field glasses. We had a great view of everything that happened. The 8th Marines' attack went like clockwork. It was really a pleasure to watch fresh, well-trained marine fire teams at work. The fire teams went out—some men rushing, some providing covering fire—and then the tanks came rolling through. They were doing just fine, especially after sitting on a ship for a month. They must have been ready to do something. You could see that everybody knew everybody else. They went right on through their objective with hardly a pause, and with relatively minor casualties. *Bing, bing, bing*—just like clockwork. The next day they secured the island.

Like I said earlier, I thought the V Amphibious Corps made a major error by deciding not to land a fresh 3d Marine Division regiment two weeks before Iwo Jima was secured. I think the island would have fallen to them in only a few days and with much fewer marine casualties. By the third or fourth week on Iwo, the troops were like zombies. They did not recognize anyone because all the familiar faces were gone, replaced by new officers and men. Units were moving as though they were in a deep sleep. I'm convinced that could have been avoided by sending the 3d Marines ashore. They would have gone through the remaining Jap positions there like the 8th Marines did on Okinawa. It was just too bad.

The ultimate irony for me was that I had volunteered to leave beautiful Maui to take command of a battalion on Okinawa, only to find that the man I was supposed to replace had not been hurt. Jeb Stuart was ill, but he did not feel inclined to turn over the battalion before the battle ended. When he asked me to be his executive officer, I accepted, even though I had studiously avoided that job throughout the entire war. But Jeb was good to his word: he turned the battalion over to me after the battle and left for the States and a lengthy stay in a navy hospital. I fully expected that I would get to lead it in the invasion of Japan.

■   ■   ■

We had only about seven tanks running at the end of the battle. We moved into an encampment up north on the Motubu Peninsula, towing a number of our disabled tanks with us, although we expected to receive new ones soon in preparation for the invasion of the Japanese home islands. We did not know it yet, but the III Amphibious Corps was not scheduled for the November invasion of Kyushu, which was code-named Operation Olympic. Instead, we would participate in a much bigger assault: Operation Coronet, which called for a landing on the Kanto Plain near Tokyo in 1946. That explains why we did not see any new tanks right away, and why the division was left alone on Okinawa to mend itself and train replacements. I was glad to see the bomb end the war, though. It was best for all of us, Japanese and Americans alike, that the fighting ended.

At this point, I began to labor over a very big decision in my life: Should I continue serving in the Marine Corps or return to civilian life now that the war was over? I was twenty-seven years old and had survived the Second World War. Marine Corps headquarters sent a letter to all officers below the grade of colonel asking it they wanted to remain on active duty or go inactive. The Corps had to know for planning, but we were given only a few days to respond. They were asking us to make a major life decision very quickly, even though most of us were far from loved ones who would be affected by our choice. I was in touch with Bob Reed on Maui, and he was asking me what we were going to do, apropos of our earlier agreement made aboard ship after Iwo. At this point, I could see it both ways. I had spent almost my entire adult life as a Marine Corps officer and was eligible for promotion to lieutenant colonel in a few months. Promotions were later delayed for several years, but I did not know that yet. There was every possibility that I could have a successful career in the Corps, extending through retirement. I loved the Marine Corps. It was like being in a fraternity of wonderful guys. On the other hand, only having been in the Corps, I had a desire to see what else was out there in the world.

I tried to make the decision in a meaningful, scientific way. I took a pad of yellow paper, and drew a big T on it to list pros and cons. However, before I put down any reasons, I asked myself for the first time, Neiman, what in the hell do you want to do for the rest of your life? I thought about it for a little while and came up with an answer that made the rest simple. What I really want most out of life, I said to myself, is to go home to the United States, meet some *beautiful* girl, fall in love, have her fall in love with me, get married, and raise a family. Then I said to myself: If that's what you want, Neiman, your decision should be easy. I can't think of a worse place in which to do that than in the USMC.

I immediately wrote Reed a letter using V-mail so it would get to Maui in a day or two. I told him I had decided to go on the inactive list. He quickly responded that he was going to do the same. My letter through channels said that I would like to go inactive as soon as it was convenient for the Corps. I guess most of us must who had survived the war felt that way in those days. Bob and I had also talked about living in Southern California. We had really fallen in love with the Los Angeles area and its lifestyle. We loved the climate and the informality. It was an open society, not structured in old hierarchies the way even small-town life was back East. Everything in Southern California seemed open and fresh. It seemed like everybody was from somewhere else, so it did not matter where. At least that is what it seemed almost sixty years ago. Continuing in the Marine Corps would surely mean giving up on that dream. It also meant that we would never find out what our potential was in other civilian pursuits. That was it. I would leave the Corps, but stay in the reserves while I set out to make my fortune in the business world—for which I had been preparing before I entered the 1st Officer Candidate Class in 1940.

After Reed and I decided what we were going to do, I went to the division personnel office and filled out the paperwork. About a month passed before I got word that my relief was coming and that I would be allowed to go home soon thereafter. Not long after that a wonderful guy whom I had never met previously arrived: Lt. Col. Alexander B. Swenceski, who had commanded the 2d Tank Battalion at Tarawa. His landing craft blew up before hitting the beach and he spent the rest of the war in a hospital. Now recovered, he had been sent to take over my battalion. He arrived just as my orders to go home were being cut at division headquarters. At the same time, we learned that our amphibious corps—which consisted of the 1st and 6th Marine Divisions and the 1st Marine Aircraft Wing—would be going to China to supervise the

Japanese surrender there and to act as a security force during their re-
patriation. The mission involved keeping the Chinese from taking ven-
geance on the Japanese, and securing the Japanese weapons so they did
not fall into the wrong hands. "Bob you are leaving at the wrong time,"
said Swenceski, who had served in the 4th Marines in China before the
war. "You've got to go to China. You will really enjoy the experience."
I agreed, saying that it had to be a lot better than Okinawa, Iwo, and the
rest of those stinking islands I had been on except for Maui. "I'd like to
go to China," I added. "But how in the hell can I do that? You're taking the battalion, so what can I do?" He looked at me and said, "You
can be my exec." I held up my hand and interjected, "Only if it's un-
derstood that I'm not going to do any work, I'm just going along as a
tourist." He said, "That's fine, it'll be great."

As luck would have it, the 1st Marine Division's deputy of operations
officer was Lt. Col. Ray Schwenke, who had been my buddy in Bill
Buse's 1st Scout Company in 1941. I told Ray exactly what I had in
mind, and he took care of changing my orders so I would remain with
the division for the deployment to China as the executive officer, helping to turn over the 1st Tank Battalion to its new commander. "Okay,"
he said. "Just tell me when you want to go home and I'll cut new orders for you."

Ray also passed along to me a curious postscript to my long relationship with Louie Jones, who had wanted to court-martial me on Roi-
Namur and who had hounded me to take my tanks over the steep cliff
on Saipan. Jones left the 4th Marine Division after Saipan, and was promoted to brigadier general. He was now serving as the 1st Marine
Division's assistant commander. When I first ran into Schwenke, he
said: "Bob, was Louis Jones ever a tank officer? We've been trying to
figure it out. Ever since we heard you were coming here, he's been telling everybody on the staff that you were his best tank officer." Apparently he had made a lot of flattering remarks about me to the division
staff. I could only conclude that a lot of his bluster had been a put-on,
and that he had liked me after all.

Although I had told Al Swenceski that I did not want to do any work,
it was simply impossible at the time. We had been alerted for a movement, and we had very few serviceable tanks on hand. We managed to
patch up thirteen of our M4A2 tanks, mainly by cannibalizing the disabled tanks we had dragged to the Motubu encampment. The 1st Tank
Battalion, at Jeb Stuart's insistence, was the only marine battalion

permitted to keep the twin-diesel Shermans in service in 1945. Unfortunately, there were no others on island. We called Jeb at Headquarters, where he was running the "Tank Desk." He told us that our new tanks had been shipped the previous month. He gave us the ship's name and said Guam and Okinawa were its only ports of call and said that if the tanks were not on Okinawa, they had to be on Guam. Major General Dewitt Peck, our new division commander, was worried about getting the tanks in time and sent me to Guam to look for them. I flew there and reported to Maj. Gen. Keller Rockey, the new III Amphibious Corps commander, and explained to him what I was doing. He called in an old, grizzled marine gunner and told him to take me wherever I wanted to go and help me out. He said the gunner knew the island better than anybody.

General Rockey did me a great favor with that, for I had no idea where I was going. It turned out that the island was jammed with new and old material in various dumps and depots. Although it seemed almost certain that our tanks were here, I again found little information or assistance. The officer in charge of the 5th Depot, which supposedly controlled all of the matériel on the island, said he had no tanks on receipt, and seemed to resent that fact that I was even asking to look around.

We stopped to see Lt. Cols. Holly Evans and Bob Denig, who commanded the 3d and 6th Tank Battalions, respectively, on Guam. They agreed that our tanks had to be at the 5th Depot. I telephoned General Rockey from Denig's office and explained the situation to him. I also told him that the lieutenant colonel in charge of the 5th Depot had refused to allow me to make a thorough search of the place, insisting that he had no tanks. Rockey ordered me to return to the depot and have the commander call him. I did just that—and then had to watch that poor creature while Rockey read him the riot act. The general made it clear to him that we were to search every square foot of that depot until we found those tanks.

And find them we did, resting safely under camouflage netting: sixty brand-new M4A3s fitted with 105-mm howitzers instead of 75-mm tank cannons! I thought, this can't be our newest Marine Corps tank, but it was indeed so. Some genius on the Marine Corps staff had ordered these vehicles to replace our tanks for the rest of the war. I found out later that they were the only M4s still in production in 1945, and that headquarters had force-fed them to the Fleet Marine Force over many protests. This had all been decided in late 1944 when I was still a company commander, and I was just now seeing the fruits of those decisions. I was appalled. The 105-mm howitzer was a fine artillery piece, but it had no place in a tank. You needed a high-velocity cannon to take out other tanks and pillboxes.

None of that mattered now. There was no time to be wasted. It was too late to prepare the tanks for shipment to Okinawa in time for the division's departure. I returned to Okinawa as soon as arrangements had been made to ship them to us in China. We would leave Okinawa with our older but better-armed M4A2s—very understrength, but full of the spirit of seasoned veterans looking for a new adventure.

CHAPTER 10
A China Fling
1945–46

Shipping out to China with Al Swenceski turned out to be a great idea. Al's background as an old China hand made him a perfect companion. The 1st Division convoy arrived at the Taku Bar, which guards the entrance to the Hai River. No oceangoing ships can pass over the sandbar. Even sampans have to await high tide to do so. We had to off-load all of our cargo into sampans or barges for the final leg into Tientsin (present-day Tianjin). Al came to me, saying, "C'mon Bob, we'll go ashore, take a jeep and get ahead of the rest of them by two or three days." We took a driver and set off, armed with carbines and pistols only, along with a little extra ammo. It was maybe a little foolhardy, as the division did not know if we would have to fight Japanese or communists or, on the other hand, if we would be welcomed. However, we did not worry much about it. Swenceski knew China well and was anxious to get back to it, and we headed for Tientsin, about forty miles away, on a route he knew from Taku. There was a village at nearly every crossroad, and the whole town usually turned out to greet us, everybody clapping with horizontal arms the way they do, and waving miniature U.S. flags. I don't know how they got those; maybe they had been waiting for us for some time.

Finally, Al said we were getting close to Tientsin. "How do you know that?" I asked. He replied, "Can't you smell it?" And it was true: a city of several million with such primitive sanitary services does have a distinctive odor. Crossing over the next rise we saw the skyline: It was the largest commercial city in North China, second only to Peiping (Beijing today) in size. Our hearts jumped to our throats when we spotted a fully armed Japanese infantry company marching toward us. They marched in parade-ground formation, with officers on the right side with swords at the carry. We counted about 250 men shouldering rifles with fixed bayonets. These were the first live Japanese troops I had seen who were not either shooting or surrendering after an island battle. Al and I decided that if they were going to get us we would take a few of them along, so we loaded and cocked our weapons and drove along, holding the carbines low at our sides. As we approached, the commanding officer yelled a command. We did not know if it was "Kill those bastards!" or what, and we were feeling pretty itchy ourselves. A couple of seconds later, he yelled another command. This time all the officers brought their swords up to salute and the troops presented arms. We saluted back as we passed. As soon as we were clear, he shouted the order to carry on and they resumed their march.

We entered the city soon after that. Swenceski wanted to find the girls' high school in the Japanese concession, as he vaguely remembered that it would be a good place for a tank park. We did not find it right away, and it was getting dark fast. There is a great nightclub called the Forum, in the Italian concession. There had been no U.S. concession in Tientsin in the old days, but France, Britain, Russia, Japan, Italy, and Germany had had them ever since the Boxer Rebellion. This resulted in problems with street names. For instance, Tientsin's main street in the British concession was Victoria Boulevard. It became the Rue de Maréchal Foch in the French area, the Via Garibaldi in the Italian area, and so on, as it wound through the city.

Al said we could eat, drink, gamble, and watch jai alai at the Forum. We parked our jeep right in front, next to a uniformed Chinese doorman. Al went over to the man, pointed to his pistol and then to the jeep, and said in pidgin Chinese that the jeep had better be there when he came out. We went inside carrying our pistols and carbines and looking none too clean, and entered a very elaborate ballroom setting. The guests were all Europeans, the men in tuxedos and the women in gowns. Heads turned in our direction and silence fell over the room. They were scared to death, and did not know what would happen. Swenceski went up to the bandleader and asked if he spoke English. He said he did. "Okay," said Al. "I want the microphone." He then turned to the crowd and said: "We are troops of the United States. We are U.S. Marines here to bring peace to North China. We have been assigned to Tientsin to bring peace to the area, repatriate the Japanese, and remain until the Chinese government can take over. You have nothing to fear from us. We are here tonight to enjoy this lovely club."

Everybody applauded, and the maître d'hôtel came over to offer his services, seats for jai alai, and so forth. The only booze they had was Johnny Walker Red, so we drank that and watched jai alai, which I had never seen before. We ate a great dinner, but the question of where we would spend the night remained. Swenceski asked the maître d' if the rooftop garden was still there. It was, so we decided to use the Forum's bathroom to clean up and then slept in our sleeping bags in the rooftop garden. The Chinese doorman slept in our jeep and guarded it.

The next morning we went out and again looked for the Japanese high school. Japanese troops had used it as a barracks, so we went to the commander's office. He spoke English, and we told him to get his troops out that day. We explained that they would eventually be assigned to a prisoner of war (POW) compound, but they had to vacate the school now. Then we made a big sign saying "1st Tank Battalion, 1st Marine Division," and hung it outside. At that point, we did not know that the plumbing did not work. We never did find out whether it had just deteriorated or the Japanese sabotaged it just before we took over. Regardless of how it happened, it became a big problem. The school's large playground provided plenty of room for our vehicles, and that was why we wanted it. Unfortunately, we later wound up having to dig latrines there as well. We now planned to sleep in the billeting area of the school. We left the jeep and driver there and took rickshaws around town.

That night, we passed a very good-looking girl on the sidewalk. By the time we were able to get our driver to turn around, she was no longer there. It was not a wasted effort, though, as we found ourselves in front of a nightclub. We were in the French concession, and the club's name in French meant "Golden Shoe." A former horse jockey owned it. We stepped down four steps to the front door and went inside. There was a small dance floor with a combo playing, and a big bar. We figured the pretty girl we had seen must be here somewhere, and indeed she was. We introduced ourselves. We had no real problem, as the word was out on us. We sat down in a booth and ordered drinks. We later met her brother, the assistant proprietor. He was anxious to please, and produced what he said was the best scotch in China: Johnny Walker Red, of course. We drank and got to know the girl, a gorgeous White Russian named Tuba. She soon became my girlfriend.

■   ■   ■

The battalion arrived the next morning, and we got to work. We knew we needed latrines dug, Lister bags for drinking water, field telephones, and many other services. We had no washing facilities, however. The sergeant major called me a day later to tell me that a nice young Chinese man had come in to offer the use of the Tientsin YMCA for showers. It was like manna from heaven; I was delighted. I told him to make the deal, and then bring the man over afterward, so that I could thank him. When the "nice young Chinese man" arrived at my office, he was dressed in western-style clothing, the first Chinese I had seen that way, and spoke excellent English. I was intrigued, but first I asked if his facility had a basketball court. It did, so I struck a deal to use it and then proceeded to ask where he had learned to speak English so well. He said he had gone to an American university in Peiping. It was a missionary school run by a Reverend Stuart for the kids of diplomats and wealthy Chinese. He told me that his father and uncles had all gone to school in the United States. His father and an uncle attended Yale, and the father had continued on to Harvard Medical School and then graduate medicine studies at Columbia University. I later learned that his father was the leading doctor in North China. He said his other uncle studied architecture at the University of Chicago and that his older sister had also studied in the states. I asked where, and to my utter surprise, he said she had graduated from the University of Maryland in 1937. I knew immediately who she was: there had been only one oriental girl in the student body, and everybody knew her. She was a predental student, and had graduated two years ahead of me. He confirmed that she was now a dentist. I then made this coincidence known to him, and we promptly went to her office in a staff car. We had a nice reunion, even though we had not known each other closely at the university.

The Kwan family officially received us in their home. They lived in a tremendous house with a gorgeous living room designed by the architect uncle. The ceiling was made of inlaid wood that had been fabricated in the United States and shipped to Tientsin. It became my home away from home. Before I left, several months later, Mrs. Kwan gave me a four-hundred-year-old Ming Dynasty gown for my mother. It had gold thread on velvet and other intricate embroideries, and my mother often wore it to parties.

Doctor Kwan wanted to throw a big party for the Allied brass, and I was the conduit to get the right people there. He asked that I be sure to include some British officers, who by then were in the city. I put together a list of all the colonels and above—and me, of course. I looked for Mrs. Kwan and her daughter at the party, but they were nowhere to be seen. I found John, the brother, and he told me that it was a formal occasion, and women were not invited. Mother Kwan had supervised the preparation of the meal, but the women had then repaired to their quarters. The guests began to take seats around several round tables, and the stewards brought in big bowls of things. There were three different bowls on each table, entrées I guessed, and you served yourself from each. After those three bowls had been removed, the servants returned with three more bowls. If you were really stupid, like me, you took some from each of these as well. Then another three bowls appeared. There must have been thirteen entrées, and long before the end I developed an incredible pain in my stomach, which was being stretched to the extreme. I thought it would be discourteous not to eat some of everything. It was a marvelous meal, but I was greatly relieved when it ended.

We found a wonderful place to live in the city. Al wanted an apartment in the British concession overlooking Victoria Park, and we discovered one on the side of the park opposite Victoria Boulevard. The buildings were all across the street from the park, a long line of luxury apartment-houses, each three or four stories high. Each story had a terraced apartment, and ours had two bedrooms, a dining room, living room, kitchen, and two baths, plus a wonderful terrace with a view of the park. Al knew of this apartment from his service there before the war, and when we first went to look at it we discovered that two Japanese colonels occupied it. We had them moved out to a POW camp and took over. We found our two houseboys shortly thereafter. The first one spoke a little Pidgin English. His name was "Cow." He then found the number-two boy. He was called "Chow," and could speak no English. Cow was also a very good cook. He would shop at the market and cook for us each day. I will never forget the time I told Cow that my favorite dessert was apple pie with cheese and asked if he could bake an apple pie. He smiled and said he made the best apple pie in the world. When he served it, we discovered the damn cheese had been cooked inside the pie and it tasted terrible. Swenceski agreed that there was no use trying to change him, as it would remain the same no matter whom we hired. So we asked for no more apple pie.

■   ■   ■

My social life became a little strained near the end. The British had maintained a large country club that was taken over by the Japanese during the war. The Marine Corps garrison took it back and converted it to an Allied officers' club. We assigned a large POW detail to clean it up and get it in shape. The main building was huge, with several restaurants, several bars, card rooms, and the like. Outside, a big racetrack dominated the property. We later accepted the surrender of a Japanese armored unit there. The Japanese had kept up and used the racetrack. All of the Europeans in town waited anxiously for the club's reopening because it was bound to be a gala event. Meanwhile, I had been going out with Tuba, the White Russian girl I met at the Golden Shoe club. I did not find out until several weeks later that she was married to the proprietor, the little jockey. She was very attractive, however, and we seemed to get along really well. I took her to many places, and we had a lot of fun together.

The 1st Marine Division had a 10 P.M. curfew for the enlisted men, which meant that the clubs emptied out then. Swenceski and I would take a nap until about eight in the evening, get up, shower, and leave at ten to go to the Golden Shoe. There we would have dinner with Tuba. After drinking, eating, and dancing, I sometimes took her to my apartment—after which I would take her to where she and the jockey lived. One night, not long before the opening of the Allied officers' club, she told me that we would have to stop seeing each other because her husband was becoming suspicious. He usually locked up the club at about 2 A.M., closed the books, and then headed for home. Up to that point I had managed to get her home before he returned, but now she told me that we had to end it because he was very, very suspicious. I told her that I would like to allay those suspicions for her benefit later and asked if she thought getting them both invitations to the big event would help. She said she thought that it might, so I did. When the great occasion arrived, Al and I sent our command car to fetch them and Al's girl, brought them to our apartment where we had drinks, and then we were driven to the club.

As we were registering our guests, I saw one of our company commanders, Capt. John Gaiesky, walking away from the desk. The girls said they wanted to go to the powder room, and after they left I went to the men's room with the French jockey following along right behind me. Gaiesky, who was already loaded, came out as I started to enter the men's room and said to me in a very loud voice, "Major, who is that goodlookin' broad you're with?" I figured, boy, I better stifle this right away, so I said, "Oh, she's the wife of a very good friend of mine," hopefully loud enough for my guest to hear. But John cut me off, saying, "Don't give me any of that baloney, all I want to know is are you getting any?" I repeated what I said, and he responded by repeating what he said. I glowered at him and said, "Get lost." Unfortunately, the damage had already been done. When we got back to the girls, the atmosphere was somewhat chilly. Shortly after that, the new French consul general introduced us to some new girls, who had just arrived from Paris.

Years later, Suzy and I ran into a White Russian couple running a very fine restaurant on Sunset Boulevard in West Hollywood, where Spagos is now located. The couple that ran it came from Shanghai but had lived in Tientsin before moving there in the 1930s. Both of their parents had operated fine restaurants in Shanghai's French concession, on opposite sides of the same square. They were forced to leave in 1949 when the Communist Chinese took over. As we talked I discovered that they knew Tuba, my White Russian girlfriend in China, and they told me she had gone to Brazil. Later, when I told them that Suzy and I would be visiting China in 1979, they asked us to take pictures of their old restaurants so they could see what had become of the buildings. The Chinese had changed the names of the streets, of course, but I managed to orient myself. At first, nobody would tell us where the street I was looking for had been, least of all the official guide we had been given. While we were in Shanghai, we stayed at one of the oldest hotels in what had been the French concession. Finally, the elderly Chinese doorman told us in hushed tones where the street was. The street we were looking for was just a block away from the hotel, and from there it was another ten blocks to the square. It was obvious which buildings had housed the two restaurants, although one had been converted into a sewing factory and the other a vegetable store. We took pictures of both buildings, plus several more of the surrounding neighborhood, and brought them back—much to the delight of the White Russians on Sunset Boulevard.

■　■　■

A large plaque honoring a marine captain named Worton hung on a wall behind the bar in the former British country club in Tientsin. His full name was William A. Worton, and he was with us in China as a brigadier general serving as General Rockey's chief of staff. The plaque, which had been placed there by the British in the 1930s, recognized his accomplishments with Tientsin's marine garrison.

John Kwan helped me a lot before I left China. I wanted to buy things for my parents, and he said he would help me find some real bargains, but that I should wait until I was ready to leave because of the currency inflation. When I arrived in China, the dollar was worth sixteen hundred Chinese dollars, and it was steadily rising. The morning of the day before I left, John took me to a most curious curio shop that was several stories high. He told me to look around the ground floor but not to buy anything. The most interesting stuff was upstairs, he said, but the old man did not want to sell any of it until it was clear a customer was not going to buy any of the goods on the ground floor. "We'll have to look at it all," he explained, "but make it clear that you don't like anything. Furthermore, if you find something you like when we go upstairs, let me know and I'll tell you if it's genuine or not. If it is, don't pay it any more attention, just look at other things and ask their prices. Then, at the end, make a casual inquiry about the item you really want." We wound up spending the entire day compiling a long list of items we wanted. However, I had only U.S. dollars, which everybody up to that point had been glad to take. But this old man said he did not understand U.S. money and he refused to take it. I could not believe it. It was after four and the banks were closed. I told him I would find a moneychanger and convert my dollars to Chinese currency. When I got out and found the changer, I discovered that the exchange rate had jumped from 2900:1 to perhaps 3600:1 during the day. The bargains thus turned out to be even better than I had first thought.

The 5th Marines provided our garrison in Peiping. We regularly sent a truck convoy to that city over a low mountain range on a winding road. It then continued on the flat plateau to Peiping. It was a routine mail and supply run, carrying drivers only for the most part. Nothing strange happened for several weeks, but one day the convoy was stopped in the hills by a tree that had fallen across the road. It did not occur to anyone that it was deliberate, and while the drivers tried to remove the obstacle they came under fire. They immediately jumped back in their trucks and hightailed it back to Tientsin. They had no radios because this was supposed to be a peaceful movement. General Peck ordered a plane from the air wing to check out the area, but the pilot saw nothing. Division headquarters decided to send an escorted convoy to counter the presumed bandits. We assigned a tank platoon to the escort detail, almost half the tanks we had available. Al asked me to go along, so I took charge. I placed a dozer tank in the lead and followed it in my jeep, with the rest of the tanks interspersed among the trucks, with the last tank bringing up the rear. I had a radio and I brought the lead driver of the previous detachment with me. He pointed out the tree to us, still unmoved. I told the lead tank to push through, which he did. A burst of small-arms fire erupted from the right. I jumped in a tank and all of us swung our guns toward a hill about five hundred yards away. We saw some of the bandits, and they appeared to be armed only with rifles. A couple of volleys of 75-mm fire sent them running. A few of us then went to the spot where they had been and found spent cartridge cases scattered all around the position. We decided to leave three of the tanks there, surrounded with concertina wire we had brought in one of the trucks, and sent the convoy on with the remaining tank section. From that time on, we sent tanks with each convoy. But the forty- or fifty-mile trip was a lot for those old, worn-out vehicles, so we relayed them by sections in and out of the camp to either Tientsin or Peiping so that no tank had to cover the full distance in a single run. I learned later that somebody touched the wire the first night the three tanks were there, setting off the noisemakers hung on the wire. The tanks lit up their headlights and fired machine guns in the direction from which the sound came. They killed a couple of intruders and the camp was not disturbed anymore. Eventually, a company of Nationalist Chinese troops arrived to take over the camp. We pointed out to the company commander and his officers the positions we had occupied and where the bandits' fire had come from, and finally gave him a map with both positions marked on it. They later received some of our tanks when the new M4A3s arrived. The communists later captured the position, which may explain why an old M4A2 is now reportedly in the Beijing military museum.

■ ■ ■

The Japanese had maintained a huge army in North China, some of which was withdrawn from Manchuria when the Russians attacked. Among the many units was the 3d Armored Division. The Japanese assumed we had a comparable armored unit in our forces and the Japanese division and assistant division commanders came forth and announced that they wanted to surrender to the commander of the American armored unit, which was Al Swenceski. "Let's do it," said Al. We lined up our thirteen operational tanks along one side of the racecourse. The Japanese kind of passed in review by us and lined their hundred or so vehicles along the other side, going around the curve. As the vehicles parked, the crews piled out and formed up at attention while the rest of their vehicles took their positions. The 1st Marine Division band played, and we had an interpreter. The two generals marched out and Al and I did the same. We met them in the center of the racetrack's infield. The generals surrendered their swords to us (I still have mine), and the interpreter related to us the history of the family swords as told by the generals. A marine military police detachment marched off the troops, who had all dismounted from their vehicles. We had a fairly large audience, including the newly arrived French consul general, the 1st Marine Division staff, and many other onlookers. When the consul general asked to see the inside of an American tank, I offered to show him and also give him a ride around the racetrack. As I was explaining how things worked, he wondered aloud how the Japanese could have dared to oppose us with their puny light vehicles. Afterward, he invited me to the reopening of their consulate. I accepted and it was a great party. At about the same time, I received orders to return to the United States.

Officers and tanks from a Japanese tank regiment that surrendered at Tientsin.

■ ■ ■

The night of the French consul general's big party, I was the junior Marine Corps officer present. I pretty much had my choice of the French girls brought over for the new consulate. Champagne flowed freely, and large platters of food were brought out. I went back to the apartment early in the morning and found that my two Chinese houseboys, Cow and Chow, had packed all of my gear. We got in the command car with Swenceski to go to the port, and there they "poured" me onto the fantail of the sampan going out to the Taku Bar. The two boys pleaded with me to take them, which I surely would have liked, but I had to explain that it simply was not possible. As I went down the river, we passed the M4A3 tanks mounting those damned 105-mm howitzers coming up in barges from the Taku Bar. I had been in China for four months, which is how long it took for the depot in Guam to "immediately" ship those tanks!

The ship that I boarded was an old attack transport. We were classified as "casuals," which meant we did not belong to a single unit. There were maybe forty or fifty of us in all, including four officers, with me being the senior. All of us came from the 1st Marine Division, and we became good pals during the trip. I had chosen this ship because Ray Schwenke told me it was going to San Francisco. I had fine memories of San Francisco from my return there in 1942, and I wanted to repeat the experience—so much so that I skipped taking another ship scheduled to travel through the Suez Canal to New York City. You can imagine my disappointment when, about a day out from the U.S. coast, the skipper informed me that we would be going to Seattle because there was a dock strike in San Francisco. Thanks to a bastard named Harry Bridges who had called the strike, I was going to miss going out on the town there.

My final objective was Los Angeles. I wanted to visit friends there before going to New York to see my parents, and Seattle was about as far away as I could get. The captain tried to console me, saying, "Bob, you're lucky that we are going to Seattle instead of San Francisco." He then went on to extol the beauty of the Strait of Juan de Fuca, the Puget Sound, Mount Rainier, and other sights. "You're going to go down the most beautiful stretch of water in the world, with snowcapped mountains on either side. You'll love it, and Seattle is a lovely town."

In reality, we passed through the Strait of Juan de Fuca in the dark, with a hard rain falling, and entered Seattle in a downpour. Because of the number of San Francisco–bound ships that had been diverted to Seattle, we could not even pull alongside the pier. We anchored out in the bay, where it was raining pitchforks, and the captain told us he had to unload that night and sail the next day. I protested that we could not unload in the rain, but he insisted. A number of small boats ferried us in through the sheets of rain. To get to the navy pier we had to throw our seabags over the sides of a couple of LCMs that had been tied together and clamber aboard them one after the other, then onto the dock, all in a miserable rain. There we were, about fifty officers and men standing soaked on the edge of the dock, with no one to greet us. I saw a lighted entry to a warehouse thirty or forty yards away and went over to investigate. Fortunately, the door opened. I motioned for the men to come over and led them inside out of the miserable rain. I was still the senior officer and had to take care of them. I was looking out the door a while later and saw a jeep approaching. I waved it down and, as luck would have it, the occupants were marines on shore patrol. I explained what had happened, and one of them exclaimed: "We'll take care of that right away, sir. We've been expecting you." They immediately radioed the duty officer, who sent two covered trucks to take us to the marine barracks. There they gave everybody a complete change of clothing, hot showers, and rousted the cooks to prepare a hot meal. The administrative people told me and the other officers that they would send us to the navy hotel in downtown Seattle that served as transient officers' quarters.

It was not a new hotel. The telephone in my room hung on the far wall. That ought to give you an idea of its vintage. At that point, however, it seemed very comfortable. I had a hot shower and went to bed. We four had agreed to meet for lunch the following noon in the lobby. After we ate, I made it my first task to buy a USMC trench coat and an extra set of major's leaves. We went to the Marine Corps administration office at the naval air station to look for orders. They told us that our records were in San Francisco and that we would have to wait several days for our discharges to be processed. They told us to enjoy ourselves and wait for their call to process our terminal leave when our records arrived.

■　■　■

Back at the hotel, we decided to meet for cocktails, but then we found that Seattle did not have any bars—Washington was a dry state! You had to buy a bottle from one of the state-run liquor stores and go to a private home to drink it—or be a member of a private club. The state stores had limited hours of operation, so we needed to make our move quick. The hotel had a concierge for the officers' billeting service. It was manned by a couple of cute USO volunteers. One of them told me that the best place in town for a drink and dinner was the Italian Club. She said the manager was a close friend, and that she would call him to see if he would take care of us. She gave us the address, and we took a cab. The manager greeted us in the reception area and had the reception girl take our personal information. He then gave us a week's honorary membership so that we could use the club facilities. He also offered to renew our membership if we were still there after a week.

We went inside and found a large cocktail lounge. There was a long bar on the left, and a series of tables scattered around. We picked a table and, as this it was already 5:30 P.M., started drinking martinis. We felt like we were in seventh heaven. We were dry, clean, shaved, and had a week of liberty. The room beyond the bar was the dining room, and there was an illegal casino in the room after that. The casino was the main reason the club existed, but we never went into it except to take a look.

Anyway, we were enjoying our drinks, the first we had had since leaving China, when in came a middle-aged lady—a nice looking woman in her forties—accompanied by three young girls of perhaps nineteen or twenty. They, too, were nice looking; not beautiful, but very nice. We had already had a number of drinks, and we decided we should meet them. We introduced ourselves and discovered that the older woman was yet another White Russian. We pulled up chairs and it became one big party. A short time later we invited the ladies to dinner—by then thoroughly drunk—and the dining room quickly filled.

We began leading the people in singing the "Marines' Hymn," and other songs. At that point, I was beginning to think that even though we had not made it to San Francisco, this was not half bad. We reminisced about China, and then one of the girls suggested we go someplace to dance. She also told us that we had to have our own bottle. We barely made it to the liquor store, which closed at 10 P.M. After picking up the booze, the girls took us to a second-story place that was kind of like a speakeasy. We had a good bottle, but I cannot remember if we got anything good served to us. The place had a little dance floor and a small combo. The drinks they served us supposedly came from our bottle. After choosing a table, we danced. After we had a couple of drinks, the girl I was dancing with said to me, "Why don't we leave the others and go out on our own?"

So we skipped out. The girl said: "I know where we can go and have fun for a long time. They party all night." I said, "Where's that?" She said, "The Colored Elks." I did not know they had a colored Elks Club, but one of the things that happened after I got the Navy Cross was that a lot of clubs, including the Elks, had sent me honorary memberships. I still had their card in my wallet. I pulled it out and showed it to her, and she said: "Let's go! I know them there." It was a building like an old New York City row house, with steps going up a half-story, to an entranceway with two big doors. We rang the bell, and the door opened. A big, jovial, smiling doorman greeted us and I showed him my card. He smiled again, slapped me on the back, and said, "That's great, c'mon in." We entered and the smoke inside was thick enough to cut. I looked around and saw that we were the only white people among the several hundred persons there. Everybody was drinking and having a good time.

The next thing I knew, the telephone was ringing. I was in my room, and the phone on the wall was ringing. I got up and reached for it. It was the young lady with whom I had gone to the Elks Club. "We had a date for six o'clock, you know!" she snapped. I did not grasp what she was talking about. What was she doing calling me so early in the morning. However, looking at my watch, I saw that it was 6:15 P.M. the next day! "I've been waiting in the lobby for you," she said. We had apparently agreed to have dinner Sunday night. Here it was 6:15 and I was still half-asleep. She finally convinced me that we had made the agreement, and I asked for a half-hour to get ready. She agreed. I was really confused for a moment, but I then remembered the large pay advance I had drawn and had been carrying. The first thing I thought was, "My God! I've been rolled." I went to the closet, where my clothes hung. Fortunately the money was still there. However, the trench coat was missing. I had no idea where I had been or how I had gotten back to the hotel. I still do not know to this day. The girl later told me that after we had been in the Elks for a little while she had wanted to go home. She said she looked all around for me but could not find me, so she took a cab home. However, we had agreed to have dinner the next night before she lost me.

I had a date with her every night for the rest of my stay in Seattle. Finally, the last night, after we had been to a few places, she said: "Before you leave, there's one place you've got to see. We can't take a taxi because it's up an alley. We'll have to walk the last block." I said that was okay, that I was game. As we walked up the alley, I saw a big shore patrolman (SP) standing in front of the place, guarding its entrance. He was twirling his baton, watching everybody going in and out. As we approached, she told me it was a club for enlisted men, and said I would never see anything like it again. I figured the SP would try to discourage us from entering, what with me being an officer and in uniform. However, as soon as he saw us he broke into a big smile, and said, "Why, major, it's good to see you again." The girl looked at me and asked, "When were you here?" I said, "I don't know what he's talking about."

As we went inside, the SP said, " Did you ever get your coat, major?" Now, even more perplexed, I said no. The girl stared at me curiously. "C'mon in and we'll get your coat for you," he replied. I asked him how the coat got there. He said, "Well, you came in Saturday night [it was now Thursday or Friday] and you had a high-yellow on each arm." He then paused and explained to the girl I was with how good-looking they were. "Anyway," he continued, "you sat down at this table here, and you were having more fun than anybody. You took off your coat and hung it on the back of the chair. At some point you got up. I thought you were going to the head, but you never came back. When we closed the joint, I took your coat and gave it to the bartender, saying, 'Keep this for the major, he'll be back for it.'"

When he finished, we went to the bar. The girl with me was reeling. I got a big welcome from the bartender. "I knew you'd be back for it," he said, holding it out to me. There it was, insignia and all. We stayed there for a while and then I took her home. And so ended my "lost weekend" in Seattle.

Epilogue

While I was on Okinawa commanding the 1st Tank Battalion, I heard a most intriguing rumor: a B-29 bomber had dropped a huge bomb on a Japanese city, obliterating it. According to the rumor, the first bomb was followed by another B-29 dropping a similar giant bomb on another Japanese city, destroying it, too. Neither city was Tokyo. Also, according to the rumor, President Truman had said in a radio broadcast to Japan, that unless the Japanese quickly surrendered, we would drop similar bombs on many Japanese cities, including Tokyo. The rumor went on further to the effect that the Japanese were expected to surrender very soon! Now that was something I really wanted to believe, but to me it sounded too improbable to be true.

However, when I called my buddy at division operations, Lt. Col. Ray Schwenke, he confirmed the validity of the rumor and said the Japanese surrender was expected within hours. By that time it was early evening. I called all our battalion officers and staff NCOs together and told them what I had heard. I said that Ray Schwenke had promised to call our headquarters if and when the Japanese surrendered. I issued instructions that if we did receive such a call that all three of our battalion clubs—the privates' club, NCO club, and officers' club—were to be opened. The privates' and NCO clubs were to be well stocked with free beer, as much as they wanted. I also quietly informed my sergeant major that we (the officers' club) would supply them (the NCOs) with scotch and bourbon, also free, of course. We had a good supply of liquor at our battalion's officers' club, which had only recently arrived, and for which the battalion officers had paid.

Before leaving the gathering of our officers and NCOs, I told them that if the war really was ending, they must make absolutely sure no weapons were fired during the celebrating. Anyone violating that order was to be locked up until I gave the order to release him. I also told them that if the call from division came through that the Japanese had indeed surrendered, I wanted to immediately be awakened, no matter what the hour. Then I went to my tent and crawled into my "sack."

Sometime during the wee hours of the morning, I was awakened by lots of noise: boisterous singing, or rather shouting, of the "Marines' Hymn"—and it did not sound as though the noisemakers were very sober! I immediately guessed the reason for the celebration, quickly dressed, and joined the happy throng at the officers' club. My recollection is that by dawn, or soon thereafter, most of us were floating around in the East China Sea.

Over the next few days I did a lot of thinking about the war we had just survived. First, I thanked God for bringing me through it all in one piece! Then I thought about all of my good friends who had not made it through to the end. I prayed a little for them and their families. I believe I remained quite subdued for a few days. Then I seemed to recover and began to enjoy life in what I perceived to be a peaceful world. The United States had won, and I was still around to enjoy life and the yet unknown fruits of victory.

After leaving Seattle with my terminal leave papers and advance pay in hand, I went on to Camp Pendleton, where I stayed about ten days. I saw old friends, including several of the girls I had dated while I was stationed there. It was great to be back in Los Angeles, a place I had fallen in love with and where I eventually wanted to live. Los Angeles was a lovely city back in those days, not the large, overcrowded metropolis it is now. The Beverly Hills area, with its big houses and boulevards, especially attracted me. There was nothing like it in the east, and I just loved it.

I then flew back East to visit my parents and link up with Bob Reed, as we had agreed to do when I left for China. I flew on a DC-3, from Los Angeles–Burbank to New York–La Guardia. We made three stops along the way, two of which were memorable. First came Salt Lake City. It was snowing hard and the airline delayed our departure. When evening came, they decided to take us to a hotel across from the temple. However, it was full of people, many in the same plight, and they showed us to army cots in the lobby, where we were told we could sleep until they announced the flight. Sometime in the wee hours, we were awakened and told to get ready for the bus ride back to the airport. We boarded the plane and took off, but a little while later we must have caught up with the same storm, because the weather forced us to land in Des Moines.

This time, we were left sitting on the plane. Two guys pleaded to be allowed to get off because it was getting hot and very boring. They went to a liquor store and brought several bottles back. After reboarding, they started handing out booze in paper cups. The stewardess objected, but they ignored her and continued to pour drinks. In no time at all, most of the passengers were pretty well drunk. Then the pilots announced we had been cleared for takeoff and would be going to Chicago, our next scheduled stop. The flight was rough, and several people threw up all over the place. By the time we got to Chicago, the stewardess was beside herself. We soon saw why. The guy opening the exit door took one whiff and slammed it shut after taking the stewardess out. It must have been an awful smell. Then the station manager entered the plane and chewed us out royally, saying that nobody would be allowed to continue to New York City and that they were dismissing the stewardess. We protested. I told him the stewardess had tried hard to stop us and that it was not her fault. Furthermore, I said that I was going on to New York and that he could try and stop me. He decided not to push it, and I completed the trip uneventfully. A day or two later, I wrote to the president of the airline saying that the stewardess had tried hard to maintain control and should not be fired. A short time later I received a reply from him saying that she had not been fired, but I have no idea if that was true or not.

I traveled on to Mount Vernon, where I stayed with my father. Mother still had her apartment in Manhattan, and I visited her, too. They had separated in 1932, when I was fourteen years old and living at the Riverside Military Academy. In 1936, they divorced and my dad remarried. I dearly loved them both.

Buried inside the gear I had shipped back was the bottle of Japanese Suntory scotch I had liberated from the Tinian cache. I had been saving it to have with my dad if I lived through the war. I had carefully wrapped it in clothing in my footlocker, and it arrived intact, so we opened the bottle. It was my first night home, and we talked all about the war and killed that excellent bottle by the early hours of the morning.

■ ■ ■

Bob Reed was already back and living on the family farm in western Pennsylvania, as the 4th Marine Division had demobilized in November. I contacted him there, and he came to New York, where we stayed in Mother's apartment. Later in our stay, one of my dates fetched a date for Bob for an event at the Waldorf, the annual Debutant Ball. My date was a previous "deb," and perhaps the other was, too. We escorted them, taking them first to dinner at the Saint Regis Hotel, as the ball did not begin until ten. A well-known singer, Dorothy Shea, was performing at the Saint Regis, but she would not be coming on until later, so there was no cover charge yet. When we finished eating, the waiter handed me a bill for $75. I was stunned. I still had some money left from my terminal pay, and I had carefully calculated the bill in advance to verify that I could afford it. I protested, and he returned with the right bill, which was for $25! My aunt and uncle later took Reed and me to the Copacabana. I related the story to them and asked what my uncle thought about it. He said it was an old trick pulled mostly on out of towners, especially servicemen. The waiter would give them a larger party's bill, accept their payment, and then give the cashier the correct amount, pocketing the difference. When I called him on it, the waiter had simply said he goofed and then handed over the correct bill.

My first plan for life after the war consisted of returning to the life insurance business with the company I had joined before I entered the Marine Corps: the Equitable. Technically, I was still on a leave of absence from military service. However, Reed and I needed some source of income before we could go into business together. I called the Equitable, located the right person, gave him my name, and told him I was interested in working in the Los Angeles area and that I had another young marine officer was interested in doing the same. We had an interview with a vice president who liked us and accepted the idea. He told us that, by coincidence, one of the Equitable's leading agency managers—Ron Stever, who headed the Los Angeles operation—was in New York. He set up a meeting with Ron for us for the next day. It did not take us long to realize that Ron was the kind of guy we would enjoy working for, so we agreed to join his agency.

Ron offered to let Bob stay in his home in San Marino, a Los Angles suburb, until I arrived. That was a real plus, since housing in Los Angeles was very difficult to find at that time. He planned to set up a "refresher course" for us in Los Angeles. I would get $100 a week, and Bob,

Me as a major in 1946.
Author's collection.

who had no experience, would collect $75. We agreed to a certain number of hours of schooling each week, and Ron said he would train us himself. This proved to be a very fine arrangement for us because it gave us some income while we surveyed the market to determine how we wanted to spend the "rest of our lives." Bob went to Los Angeles right away, but I begged off because I had agreed to take my mother to Florida for a vacation.

I planned to stay on the East Coast for the duration of my "terminal leave," which expired in mid-April, 1946. On February 1, I took my mother to Florida for a monthlong vacation. While we were there, I met with some friends who suggested that I contact Sylvia Davidson in Beverly Hills when I got back to California. At the time, she was the executive secretary of one of Hollywood's most successful film companies. Naturally, I took Sylvia's phone number and promised to contact her.

Soon after I arrived in Los Angeles, I did contact Sylvia Davidson. She was a lovely lady about ten years older than I, and she decided to introduce me to a beautiful Hollywood girl. When my relationship with the "beautiful Hollywood girl" ended, Sylvia introduced me to a lovely and talented young actress. When that romance eventually came to an end, Sylvia said she would try one more time. "You know," she said, "three strikes and you are out!" However, she confided that she had "saved the best for last."

Her "best" turned out to be a "war widow" who had been married to a navy flyer. He had been lost in one of the early carrier battles in the South Pacific. The widow's name was Suzy Alexander, and she was indeed the best! We had a long romance, and I finally proposed on New Year's Eve, 1950. We were married in Sylvia's garden on May 13, 1951, and, more than fifty years later, we are still married to each other and still very much in love. Our marriage produced three fine boys: John, Philip, and Andrew.

■   ■   ■

Bob Reed lived temporarily with Ron Stever as planned. Later, when I arrived, Martha Young, one of my mother's oldest friends, invited us to stay with her. We had decided to try insurance as our initial partnering operation, because we would meet a lot of people and have a steady income. We were doing reasonably well, not setting the world on fire, but doing okay, when the state of California came up with the requirement for all companies to have workman's compensation insurance, either through the state or a private insurer. A lot of large, juicy contracts could be made now. We tackled that project right away. I made connections with Sears and Roebuck through a close friend who ran the Johnson Tobacco Company, a Sears subsidiary. His introduction passed me into the office of Sears's western regional director. Our goal was to sell him the Equitable's program for his entire region. The Equitable experts we called in from New York impressed him, and he said that he would choose from one of three companies, including us. I feel certain that he wanted us, but a rival company had inside connections to Sears's chairman of the board, which swung the deal for them. Although we lost out in the power play, it turned out to be the best thing for us. If we had closed the deal, we would have stayed in the insurance business and never prospered the way we later did.

What finally broke us out of the insurance business was a dinner we had with Stever and my mother and stepfather at the Huntington Hotel. The hotel's popular Sunday dinner and dance attracted almost everybody in the area. Ron was constantly taking notes on who was there, and frequently jumped up from the table to make contacts and schmooze. Reed and I were appalled that the boss never seemed able to relax, no matter how successful he was. This was not our idea of "the good life," and we resolved to move on.

We could not help observing the fantastic growth the Los Angeles area was experiencing. People were pouring into Southern California in unprecedented numbers. Housing and buildings of all kinds were in extremely short supply. Any kind of structure would be occupied as soon as it was available. Waiting lists for houses and apartments grew longer each day. Bob and I began to feel left out of this accelerating boom. We wanted to become more directly involved in this phenomenon.

"Why not go into the lumber business?" a friend asked me one day. "Then you can ride down Wiltshire Boulevard and say, 'See that building? It's got our lumber or our roofing on it,'" and so forth. We got a kick out of the idea. It made sense, and certainly related well to the Los Angeles building boom. We talked to a number of other friends, including a few contractors, who agreed it was a good idea. The question thus became: how and where? We decided that Reed would go into building materials and learn that end of the business and I would do lumber. We saw that the San Fernando Valley and Orange County were growing fast, so Bob looked for a firm in Orange County and I concentrated on the San Fernando Valley. We already had a friend who was a brick manufacturer in Orange County. He wanted to set up a department diversifying in other complimentary materials and he agreed to hire Bob to run it, knowing that he could leave and set up his own business when the time came. Meanwhile, I went to Builders' Emporium on a rainy day dressed in a suit and hat and asked Wayne Henry for a job. He said he had no places open in the office or sales. I said I would not take one in those areas if he did. I told him I wanted a job in the yard. He looked at me like I was crazy, but I managed to convince him by saying that I needed the exercise or something. Since they could always use another man in the yard, he told me to come back the next day at 7 A.M. He smiled and added, "Be sure to wear your old clothes."

■ ■ ■

After somewhat less than a year at our new jobs, we felt we had learned as much as we could working for someone else. According to plan, we left our jobs in April, 1948, and went about setting up our own small lumberyard—the Neiman-Reed Lumber and Supply Company, Incorporated—in the heart of the rapidly growing San Fernando Valley.

During the early years of our business, our Marine Corps connections frequently proved useful in unexpected but significant ways. One such instance offers a typical example of what I mean.

In 1949, our second year in business, I was in the midst of making a determined effort to sell lumber to the movie studios. Until then, our sales had been mainly to building contractors. There were nine or ten major studios in Hollywood in those days, and they each bought several million dollars worth of lumber annually. Much of what they purchased was of a higher, more expensive, grade than the lumber we sold to building contractors. It thus commanded higher prices and meant higher gross margins, so we went after that business.

It was difficult for a salesman to get inside the studio gates, however, and it took me several months to get into some of the studios and start selling them lumber. One of the largest studio's purchasing agents was particularly hard to contact. I would show up at that studio's gate once a week, present my business card to the uniformed guard, and ask him to call the purchasing agent. The result was the same every time: the man's secretary would tell the guard her boss was not buying any lumber that day. I then would ask the guard to tell her I just wanted to meet her boss and tell him about our company in hopes that at some later date he would give us a call and ask for a price quote. It was all to no avail. Even though the guard and I became good friends on a first-name basis, I just could not get inside the gate.

At that point, I received a phone call from Hal Barker, a Marine Corps officer I had known as a lieutenant at Jacque's Farm. I had seen him recently at the local Marine Corps birthday celebration, where I learned that he had become an actor at a movie studio. It turned out he worked for Twentieth Century, the same studio that I had been trying so unsuccessfully to enter. He said he was calling to tell me that a close friend of his at the studio had written the screenplay for what had just become the most successful World War II movie yet produced: *Twelve*

O'clock High, a picture about U.S. Army Air Forces bomber raids against Germany. Later, the studio had also assigned the writer to do a screenplay about the marines in the Pacific! Since the writer knew nothing about either the Marine Corps or the war in the Pacific, he expected my friend to help him. My friend said he told the writer that his former commanding officer had much more combat experience than he did and could probably help the writer better than anyone else. The writer then asked my friend to invite me to meet them for lunch at the studio. That, he concluded, was the reason for this call.

When I showed up at the studio gate at noon, the guard saw me and started to phone the purchasing agent's secretary. I told him to call Sy Bartlett, the screenwriter, instead. Over a nice lunch, I agreed to be the writer's guest for dinner twice a week for about a month while he put the story together. At each evening meeting, I would critique, for accuracy and realism only, what he had written since our previous meeting.

Finally, the story was completed. Sy phoned me the next day to ask if I could come to his office. He sounded upset. When I arrived, he said that he had some "bad news." Apparently, the Marine Corps, who's blessing the studio needed in order to shoot the picture at Camp Pendleton with real marines, had informed the studio that only an active-duty marine officer could be listed as the military adviser in the film's credits. Thus, I would not receive any recognition in the screen credits. Ironically, the Marine Corps offered Maj. Frank E. Garretson, a close friend and classmate of mine from the Quantico officer candidate course, to serve as the picture's military adviser. We had served together in the 4th Marine Division during all of its campaigns. He was a fine officer who had been awarded the Navy Cross, and he later retired as a brigadier general—one of only three members of our class to make flag (general officer) rank.[1]

I did not care at all about getting screen credit, but I did not tell that to Sy, who seemed genuinely concerned. However, when he asked if there was anything he could do for me, I said that I would appreciate an introduction to the studio's purchasing agent. He seemed relieved that I was not too disappointed, but he was puzzled by my request. I reminded him that Bob Reed and I were in the lumber business, and then told him of my many unsuccessful attempts to see the agent. He immediately got the purchasing agent on the phone and told him that he would appreciate it if he would see me. He told him about Bob Reed and me serving together in the marines and how much action we saw. He also told the purchasing agent that

I had been of invaluable help to him in putting the script together for a forthcoming movie about the marines. The agent told him that he would be happy to see me anytime, and that it really had not been necessary for the writer to phone him.

When I arrived at the purchasing agent's office, I could see he was angry, almost livid! It did not surprise me, though. I had figured when I asked the screenwriter for help that I had nothing to lose. The agent told me that during the war, when lumber was hard to get, one lumber company had gone out of its way to "take care" of the studio. Now that lumber was no longer scarce, he was "taking care" of them, and he had no intention of buying lumber from me or anybody else.

When the purchasing agent told me that, I must have lost my cool. I leaned over his desk and grabbed him by what in the Marine Corps we call the "stacking swivel" (a rifle part we relate to the second button from the top of one's shirt), and pulled him close to me. As I stood there holding his shirt, our faces inches apart, I told him that while I could understand his wanting to be loyal to a company that had taken care of him during the war, my partner and I had taken a lot better care of him—and we had done it without profit and at considerable risk! I then let go of his shirt, did an about face, and left, never expecting to see him again. I do not know who was madder: him or me.

When I returned to my office later in the day, I found a message to phone the purchasing agent. When I got him on the line, he apologized to me for what he had said earlier and invited me to his office the next day. He said he would have an order ready for me. He added that if the studio carpenters liked our lumber, there would be more orders.

Thus began what became a very successful business relationship and a fine friendship. Before long, Twentieth Century had become our best customer. When Suzy and I were married about a year later, the purchasing agent and his wife came to our wedding.

■   ■   ■

Our company continued to grow with lots of help along the way, much of it Marine Corps related. We later opened a chain of home improvement retail stores (fourteen in all) featuring every department under one roof, the first in the industry to have everything inside, including the lumber yard. We called these stores "Lumber City."

By the mid-1970s, several national companies had offered to acquire us. Finally, in July, 1981, we sold the business to a large British conglomerate.

Bob and I owed every bit of this success to our original Marine Corps partnership—which had been achieved through hard work and training, and the testing of our teamwork in combat operations with our tank company. Ironically, the Marine Corps might have short-circuited the whole effort when the Korean War began. We were in our third year of operations and had just begun to change our business orientation and move into wholesaling specialty lumber. We had both remained on the inactive list in the Marine Corps Reserve, and for a while we thought we might have to go to war again. We called Jeb Stuart, who was then serving in a key job in the Plans and Programs Department at HQMC. However, he just laughed at our concerns. "We need junior officers now," he said. "Not you old-timers!" We thus remained free to continue our business operations.

People have asked me from time to time why Bob Reed and I were so determined to go into business together, especially with our limited experience in the private sector. I always answered that we believed our Marine Corps experience had trained us well for running a civilian company. Perhaps the most important reason, however, was that we had complete trust in one another. It may sound overly dramatic to put it

Me in Thousand Oaks, California, 1978.
Author's collection.

this way, but our mutual trust had been forged under fire. We were best friends, and we had each saved the other's life at great personal risk. Working and fighting so closely together, often in very violent situations, had taught us a great deal about each other. We learned each other's capabilities and limitations. We came to realize that while we did not have identical abilities, our strengths and weaknesses complemented each other. We thought we made a great team. However, one of the most important things the Marine Corps taught us was the value of esprit de corps and how to develop it in an organization—in other words, leadership.

In the military, one has the authority to give orders that could result in a subordinate's death or maiming. That is rarely so in civilian life. However, the principles of leadership are equally useful in both worlds. In a military organization, although subordinates cannot refuse a command, leaders want people to do more than just carry out an order; they want their very best performance. If you lead properly, you do not have to push people. They will enthusiastically achieve your goals and objectives. In civilian companies, although you lack the authority to give life-or-death orders, if you run things right, your employees are going to want to do it all. If you instill pride in their company in them, if you demonstrate that you have their interests at heart as well as your own, they will feel the urge to do everything you need done and more. If they see something else that needs to be done, they will accomplish that as well. The military and civilian worlds are fundamentally the same. If you are able to develop esprit de corps in your business, all will go well. If you fail to do that, it will not. Bob Reed and I saw this as a key advantage for us because we had the same concepts of leadership. Because we knew each other so well and complemented each other's strengths and weaknesses, we had to succeed.

Sadly, just five months after we sold our company, Bob Reed had a fatal heart attack. We miss him more than we can possibly say.

APPENDIX I
Tanks in Marine Corps Service, 1940–45

Tanks in Marine Corps service performed more strictly defined tasks than in the armies of the world, including the U.S. Army. The Marine Corps doctrine for amphibious assaults against beaches defended by a determined and well-armed enemy included the requirement for other Marine Corps units to defend islands and coastlines against similar all-out assaults. Fleet experiments in 1923 identified tanks as necessary for both of these tasks.

In 1934, the Marine Corps planned to include two tank companies equipped with five-ton light tanks in each of its two proposed brigades. The vehicle selected was the five-ton, two-man Marmon-Herrington CTL-3. The 1st Tank Company, 1st Marine Brigade, was organized at Quantico under Maj. Hartnoll J. Withers (1903–83), a 1926 Naval Academy graduate, on March 1, 1937, although it remained—in terms of equipment and personnel—a mere platoon for a considerable time. The Marine Corps bought a total of thirty-five Marmon-Herrington light tanks, but the coming of World War II led to the adoption of army light and medium tanks for a variety of reasons.

The two brigades became divisions on short notice in February, 1941, and the tank battalions planned for these divisions would be light tank units containing four companies, each with eighteen tanks. The Marmon-Herringtons were assigned to the fourth company of each battalion, and the other three received army-type light tanks. Fortunately, the Marmon-Herringtons were deemed unsuitable for combat and were packed off to garrison duty in Samoa or discarded, and the 1st–3d Tank Battalions went into combat with army-issue light tanks. By the end of 1943, the Marine Corps had deleted the fourth tank company and devised a mixed tank battalion of one medium and two light tank companies. However, only the 1st and 4th Tank Battalions were organized in this way before new orders were issued that transformed all of the Marine Corps tank battalions into medium tank battalions with three tank companies each.

The improvised nature of Marine Corps tank unit organization paralleled the lack of doctrine for tank employment, which was left largely to the units to devise. Tank units at first had no experience with operating with infantry, and early actions at Guadalcanal and Tarawa highlighted these deficiencies. By the time marines landed in the Marianas in mid-1944, each division had honed the tactical principles of tank-infantry cooperation to a competent degree. Unlike combat in Europe, however, the Pacific War contained few opportunities for massing tank power, and the three-battalion assault attempted at Iwo Jima stands out as a true exception to the normal practice of employing tank companies in support of infantry regiments. Not until the end of the war did the Marine Corps attempt to codify these practices into a series of instructions and manuals that were distributed in the postwar period.

TECHNICAL CHARACTERISTICS

Marmon-Herrington CTL-3 (introduced in 1936)
Crew: 2
Weight: 9,500 lbs.; 10,900 lbs. for CTL-3A
Armor: ¼-in.
Armament: 3 .30-cal. machine guns
Engine: Lincoln V-12, 110 hp (Hercules 6 cyl., 124 hp. in CTL-3A)
Speed: 33 MPH
Range: 125 miles
Miscellaneous: Turretless tank. The prototype was fitted with one .50-cal. and two .30-cal. machine guns and band track. Only five CTL-3s were built. Five more CTL-3As were delivered in 1939 with 10.5-in. track and reinforced suspension. The CTL-3s were rebuilt in 1941 as CTL-3As and all were upgraded and became CTL-3Ms. They were used

by the 1st Tank Company, FMF, and later the tank platoons in the 1st and 2d Scout Companies. All Marmon-Herringtons were discarded in 1943. The authors located a single survivor in the American Military Museum in South El Monte, California.

M2A4 Light Tank (1940)

Crew: 4
Weight: 23,500 lbs.
Armor: 1-in. maximum in hull and turret
Armament: 1 37-mm M5 cannon and 1 .30-cal. coax machine gun in turret; 1 .30-cal. antiaircraft machine gun on turret; 3 .30-cal. machine guns in hull
Engine: Continental W-670 radial, 262 hp
Speed: 36 MPH
Range: 70 miles
Miscellaneous: Thirty-six were acquired from the army in 1940 when it became apparent that the Marmon-Herringtons could not be delivered in time. They were used by the 3d and 4th Tank Companies, FMF, which became the A Companies in the 1st and 2d Tank Battalions in 1941. The first seventeen saw action at Guadalcanal with Company A, 1st Tank Battalion—the only combat employment of the M2A4. They were discarded in 1943.

Marmon-Herrington CTL-6 (1941)

Crew: 2
Weight: 12,500 lbs. designed; 14,775 lbs. actual
Armor: ¼–½-in.
Armament: 3 .30-cal. machine guns
Engine: Hercules 6 cylinder, 124 hp
Speed: 33 MPH
Range: 125 miles
Miscellaneous: A turretless tank, it was an improved version of the CTL-3 with track and suspension components similar to the M2A4. Only twenty were built, and all were discarded in 1943 on Samoa.

Marmon-Herrington CTM-3TBD (1941)

Crew: 3
Weight: 18,500 lbs. designed; 20,800 lbs. actual
Armor: ¼–½-in.

Armament: 2 .50-cal. machine guns in turret, 3 .30-cal. machine guns in hull
Engine: Hercules DXRB diesel, 123 hp
Speed: 30 MPH
Range: 125 miles
Miscellaneous: Turreted version of CTL series tank with track and suspension components similar to the M2A4. Only five were built, and all were discarded in 1943 on Samoa.

M3 Series Light Tank (1941)

Crew: 4
Weight: 25,600 lbs.; 26,000 lbs. for M3A1
Armor: prototype had 1.5-in. frontal, 1-in. side hull, and 2-in. gun shield (first production model had 1.5-in. turret front and 1.25-in. turret side)
Armament: 1 37-mm M6 cannon and 1 .30-cal. coaxial machine gun in turret; 1 .30-cal. antiaircraft machine gun on turret; 3 .30-cal. machine guns in hull (1 in M3A1)
Engine: Continental W-670 radial, 262 hp; some were fitted with 245 hp Guiberson T-1020 9 cylinder diesel radial
Speed: 36 MPH
Range: 70 miles (90 miles diesel)
Miscellaneous: Served as the standard tank in Marine Corps tank battalions through the end of 1943. Used as a light flamethrower tank in 1943–44 as well. The M3 introduced the vertical gyrostabilizer gun mount. The M3A1 and later U.S. World War II tanks were fitted with power turrets.

M5A1 Light Tank (1943)

Crew: 4
Weight: 30,800 lbs.
Armor: 1.75-in. lower front, 1-in. side hull, 2-in. gun shield, 1.5-in. turret front, and 1.25-in. turret side
Armament: 1 37-mm M6 cannon and 1 .30-cal. coaxial machine gun in turret; 1 .30-cal. antiaircraft machine gun on turret; 1 .30-cal. machine gun in hull
Engine: Twin Cadillac V-8, 296 hp
Speed: 36 MPH
Range: 100 miles
Miscellaneous: Issued to Marine Corps tank battalions beginning in late

1943 (summer, 1943, for 1st Tank Battalion from army stocks). Saw action on Cape Gloucester and in the Roi-Namur battles. A few remained in use on Saipan. Discarded in late 1944.

M4A2 Medium Tank (1943)

Crew: 5
Weight: 66,000 lbs.
Armor: 2–4.25-in. lower front, 2.5-in. upper front, 1.5-in. side hull, 3.5-in. gun shield, 3-in. turret front, 2-in. turret side
Armament: 1 75-mm M3 cannon and 1 .30-cal. coaxial machine gun in turret; 1 .50-cal. antiaircraft machine gun on turret; 1 .30-cal. machine gun in hull
Engine: Twin GM diesels, 12 cylinder, 410 hp
Speed: 25 MPH
Range: 150 miles
Miscellaneous: Issued to the I Corps Medium Tank Battalion in 1943. Partial issue to all other Marine Corps tank battalions began in late 1943. The M4A1 with gas engine was issued to the 1st Tank Battalion from army stocks in summer, 1943. All marine tank units converted to this model in 1944. The Marine Corps remained the sole U.S. combat user of diesel-powered M4 series tanks.

M4A3 Medium Tank (1944)

Crew: 5
Weight: 66,400 lbs.
Armor: 2–4.25-in. lower front, 2.5-in. upper front, 1.5-in. side hull, 3.6-in. gun shield, 3-in. turret front, and 2-in. turret side
Armament: 1 75-mm M3 cannon and 1 .30-cal. coaxial machine gun in turret; 1 .50-cal. antiaircraft machine gun on turret; 1 .30-cal. machine gun in hull; 2-in. M3 mortar (for smoke) in turret.
Engine: Ford GAA V-8, 500 hp
Speed: 26 MPH
Range: 130 miles
Miscellaneous: Issued to Marine Corps tank battalions beginning in late 1944. All marine tank units converted to this model in 1945; 1st Tank Battalion was the last. The postwar model used was the M4A3 with 105-mm M4 howitzer. Bulldozer and flamethrower variants continued in Marine Corps service until 1959.

APPENDIX 2
Selected Documents

The President of the United States takes pleasure in presenting the NAVY CROSS to

MAJOR ROBERT M. NEIMAN,
UNITED STATES MARINE CORPS RESERVE,

For service as set forth in the following CITATION:

For extraordinary heroism as Commanding Officer of Company C, Fourth Tank Battalion, Fourth Marine Division, in operations against enemy Japanese forces on Saipan, Marianas Islands, from 15 June to 9 July 1944. Leading his company in an attack against prepared enemy fortifications and gun positions on 19 June, Major Neiman evacuated his tank when it was immobilized by fire from a large caliber gun and led the attack from a second tank until it too was rendered inoperative by a land mine. Evacuating this vehicle under heavy machine-gun and mortar fire, he resumed command in a third tank and pressed the attack, penetrating the well-entrenched hostile positions, destroying several machine-gun and mortar emplacements and inflicting heavy casualties on the Japanese. His inspiring leadership, courage, and devotion to duty upheld the highest traditions of the United States Naval Service.

For the President,
JOHN L. SULLIVAN
Secretary of the Navy

The President of the United States takes pleasure in presenting the BRONZE STAR MEDAL to

MAJOR ROBERT M. NEIMAN, UNITED STATES MARINE CORPS RESERVE,

For service as set forth in the following CITATION:

For meritorious achievement as Commanding Officer of Company C, Fourth Tank Battalion, Fourth Marine Division, in operations against enemy Japanese forces on Iwo Jima, Volcano Islands, from 19 February to 16 March 1945. Landing on the island under intense artillery, mortar, and antitank fire, Major Neiman led his men against strong emplacements, pillboxes and fortifications and, skillfully maneuvering his company on most difficult beaches, accomplished a maximum of destruction upon the Japanese and contributed materially to the establishment of the beachhead. During this operation, he led his men against a stubborn enemy for a period of twenty-five days. His professional ability, courage under fire and unwavering devotion to duty were in keeping with the highest traditions of the United States Naval Service.

Major Neiman is authorized to wear the Combat "V"

For the President,
JOHN L. SULLIVAN
Secretary of the Navy

The President of the United States takes pleasure in presenting the GOLD STAR in lieu of a second BRONZE STAR MEDAL to

MAJOR ROBERT M. NEIMAN, UNITED STATES MARINE CORPS RESERVE,

For service as set forth in the following CITATION:

For heroic achievement as Executive Officer of the First Tank Battalion, First Marine Division, during operations against enemy Japanese forces on Okinawa, Ryukyu Islands, from 8 to 22 June 1945. Demonstrating his extensive knowledge of tank tactics, Major Neiman rendered invaluable assistance to his Battalion Commander. Acting on his own initiative, he made frequent trips to front-line positions, often in the face of heavy enemy fire, to observe hostile positions and direct the attack. When deadly antitank fire stopped our tanks on one occasion, he conceived the idea of direct tank air spotting which resulted in the destruction of the Japanese guns. His leadership, cool courage and devotion to duty were in keeping with the highest traditions of the United States Naval Service."

Major Neiman is authorized to wear the Combat "V"

> For the President,
> JOHN L. SULLIVAN
> Secretary of the Navy

U.S.S. LSM-216

ACTION REPORT
22 JANUARY – 21 FEBRUARY 1945

PART I. Brief Summary.

A.1. This ship landed on Iwo Jima on Yellow Beach on Dog Day (19 February 1945) to land tanks of Company "C," 4th Bn., 4th Mar. Div. Made four (4) beachings before getting tanks off on solid ground. Ship was hit eight (8) times on second beaching but gun was silenced by rocket firing planes. Both ramp cables parted, one (1) by tank and one (1) by gunfire. Gyro, Engine Annunciators, Radio and Radar out due to hits. Brought out numerous casualties from beach. Transferred them to transports and formed up in designated LSM area. Replaced ramp cables. Ordered to Blue One Beach to evacuate casualties. Landed at 0005 on 20 February and retracted at 0100 with 24 casualties. Beach quieter at night. Departed for Saipan, with LCI-441 in tow, about 1630 on 21 February 1945.

PART II. Preliminaries.

[omitted]

PART III. Chronological Account.

A.1. Beached on right half of Yellow Beach Two at 0935 (Zone-10 time). Company Commander's tank landed, was unable to climb terrace and turned right on beach. Sand soft and tank bogged down. Landed bulldozer equipped tank which endeavored, without success, to dig it out. Recovered personnel and bulldozer and retracted at 1015, leaving one tank abandoned on beach. Ship scarred with machine gun fire and shrapnel from mortar near misses but not damaged. No casualties.

2. Reported to Yellow Control. Transferred four (4) Marine casualties (from beach) to Evacuation Control via small boat. Ordered back to Yellow Two, left half. Informed Yellow Control that beach was too steep but ordered on in. Beached on left half of beach at 1135. Dozer tank unable to scale terrace which was steep and about ten feet high. Received eight (8) hits from medium caliber gun which was silenced by rocket firing Corsairs. Gyro, Engine Annunciators, Radio and Radar out. Several men slightly cut by shrapnel. Recovered dozer tank and retracted at 1220. Had difficulty retracting. Company "C" reconnaissance man on board plus 24 beach casualties.

3. Reported to Yellow Control and then transferred casualties. Ordered back to Yellow One. Beached at 1400 but found beach unsuitable. On ramp cable parted by tank. Scout requested we shift to right about 100 yards. Retracted at 1410, spun about, and beached again at 1415. All tanks landed and got up first terrace. Second ramp cable parted by gunfire. Retracted with ramp down, at 1435. Approximately 50 beach casualties on board. Transferred them to APA-119 and APA-196. Ordered by ComLSMFlotFIVE to stand by in LSM Area Man.

4. Ordered to evacuate casualties from Beach Blue One. Beached at 0005 on 20 February and took on board 24 casualties. Retracted at 0100. Transferred two (2) critical cases to Evacuation Control LST at 0120. Transferred balance to LSV-2 about 0500 and proceeded to LSM Area Man.

B. Weather on D-Day was excellent. Visibility unlimited with sea very moderate and from north. Surf negligible. By time of night beaching for evacuation of casualties it had shifted around to southeast and was a bit heavier.

PART IV. Ordnance.

A. There was no firing by this ship due to danger of hitting own troops on beach and inability to spot enemy emplacements.

B. Enemy small arms and artillery fire were accurate. Altho there was heavy mortar fire and many near misses there were no direct mortar hits. The near misses caused damage by fragmentation, punching numerous holes in the hull above the water line. No underwater damage apparent.

PART V. Damage.

A. Damage to this ship consisted of:

1. Five (5) large holes from direct hits by medium caliber gun on starboard side of radio shack. Chart desk top, file cabinet and miscellaneous gear and equipment ruined by shell fragments. Main wireway shot out and D.C. lines to pilot house severed. Annunciator rods severed. Radio and radar equipment shot out. About eight small holes in port side of radio shack from shell fragments. One (1) hole in wave guide tubing.

2. Two (2) large holes in plating on starboard side Engine Room, upper level, from direct hits by medium caliber gun. Miscellaneous piping in Engine Room shot out, but no vital damage.

3. About fifteen small holes in plating along starboard side from near miss mortar fragments: all above water line.

4. Gyro inoperative: extent of damage not yet ascertained. Excessive vibration in both shafts, probably from damage to screws by debris on beach.

5. Numerous small holes in and damage to bulwarks, ready service boxes, life lines and other superstructure deck installations from small arms fire.

6. Two (2) life rafts badly damaged and 80% of equipment on them ruined by direct hit from medium caliber gun. 50% of equipment on three (3) other life rafts damaged by small arms fire.

PART VI. Comments.

1. Due to the nature of the beach and the loss of the first tank off, this ship found it necessary to practically explore the beach for a suitable spot to land the remaining tanks. Tank commander reluctant to risk the loss of further tanks thru hasty landing on unsuitable beach. While on beach for considerable time each beaching we were over-run with casualties from the beach who made a break for the ramp almost as soon as it dropped. This imposed a severe strain on our medical stores a we were not equipped to handle a large number of casualties, many of whom had received no treatment and some of whom were amputation cases. We exhausted our supply of plasma and battle dressings and found it necessary to utilize crew's blankets to wrap up shock cases suffering from chills. Recommend an increase in the allowance of medical supplies for this class ship and that medical department blankets be included.

2. Both ramp cables parted on final beaching to land tanks: one (1) by tank and one (1) parted by gunfire. There was heavy machine gun fire and mortar fire which made the use of the emergency ramp hoisting cable too risky to personnel so we retracted with the ramp down. It was found that we could go at standard speed in calm sea with no deck load and there was no water pushed up on deck. Proceeded well clear of beach and rigged emergency gear to raise ramp. Replaced ramp cables underway.

CHARLES P. HABER
Lieutenant, USNR
Commanding Officer

APPENDIX 3

Robert M. Neiman
Chronology

Born: September 14, 1918, Mount Vernon, New York, son of entrepreneurs in the New York City garment industry.

Age 9–10: Saint John's Military School.

Age 14: Riverside Military Academy.

Age 15–16: Roxbury Preparatory School, Cheshire, Connecticut. Graduated June, 1935.

Attended University of Maryland School of Business on fencing scholarship, class of 1939.

1939–40: Working in insurance industry, Washington, D.C.

1940: USMC officers candidate course, commissioned 1941.

1941: Platoon leader, 1st Scout Company, 1st Marine Division.

1942: Executive officer, D Company, 1st Tank battalion, New Zealand.

1942: Operations officer, Tank School, Training Command, Camp Elliott, California (San Diego area).

1943–45: Commanding officer, C Company, 4th Tank Battalion, Roi-Namur, Saipan, Tinian, Iwo Jima.

1945–46: Executive officer, commanding officer, 1st Tank Battalion, Okinawa; executive officer, 1st Tank Battalion, North China occupation.

1946: Working in insurance and lumber industries, Los Angeles area.

1947: Founded Neiman-Reed Lumber Company, Van Nuys, California.

1957: Joined Young Presidents' Organization, by invitation (later served as vice president and board member of international YPO).

1963: Founded Lumber City (later Do-It) retail chain (grew to fourteen stores) by 1980s.

1968: Joined Chief Executives' Organization; became member of board and served as president, 1978–79.

1981: Sold company; remained as president and consultant for several years.

Civic activities: Board member, San Fernando Boy Scout Council; board member and president, Big Brothers Association; board member, national and Los Angeles chapters of National Council of Christians and Jews; board member, Greater Los Angeles Chamber of Commerce; board member and chairman, San Fernando Valley Industry and Commerce Association.

NOTES

PREFACE

1. Kenneth W. Estes, *Marines Under Armor: The U.S. Marine Corps and the Armored Fighting Vehicle, 1916–2000* (Annapolis, Md.: Naval Institute Press, 2000).
2. Robert Crisp, *Brazen Chariots* (New York: W. W. Norton, 1960).
3. Keith Douglas, *Alamein to Zem Zem* (London: Faber and Faber, 1966).
4. Avi Kahalani, *The Heights of Courage* (Westport, Conn.: Greenwood Press, 1984).
5. Ralph Zumbro, *Tank Sergeant* (Novato, Calif.: Presidio Press, 1986).
6. Bertram A. Yaffe, *Fragments of War: A Marine's Personal Journey* (Annapolis, Md.: Naval Institute Press, 1999).
7. Oscar E. Gilbert, *Marine Tank Battles in the Pacific* (Conshohocken, Pa.: Combined Publishing, 2001).
8. Eugene B. Sledge, *With the Old Breed at Peleliu and Okinawa* (Novato, Calif.: Presidio Press, 1981).

CHAPTER 1. THE EARLY DAYS

1. The Marine Corps at that time had ten Marmon-Herringtons plus thirty-six of the army's M2A4 light tanks. Our two divisions did not receive their first M3 light tanks until September–October, 1941.

CHAPTER 3. FIRST ORGANIZATIONS

1. The Dionne quints were named Cécile, Yvonne, Annette, Marie, and Émilie.
2. We were previously entitled to a housing allowance for a two-room, one-bath apartment on or off base. If not, we got the allowance, which was adjusted to local conditions. The rate was $41 for the New River area, which had no housing anyway!
3. Numbered line regiments—be they infantry, artillery, or engineers—are termed "nth Marines" in the Marine Corps.

CHAPTER 4. EARLY TESTS IN THE SOUTHWEST PACIFIC

1. The strategy of the Solomons campaign owed much of its complication to the interaction of two separate commands. General Douglas MacArthur's SWPA headquarters initially planned to seize the Japanese base at Rabaul as a steppingstone to the Philippines, but later decided to bypass and neutralize it. Admiral Chester W. Nimitz's Pacific Ocean Areas command included the Solomons chain, but not New Britain, and focused mainly upon a drive through the Central Pacific to isolate the Japanese home islands.

CHAPTER 6. GEARING UP FOR THE CENTRAL PACIFIC

1. The "coax" is a machine gun, usually .30 caliber, mounted next to the main gun in the turret, firing through its own opening in the armored gun shield. The gunner aims and fires it the same as the main gun, but using a different switch-trigger combination. One often employed "subcaliber" training by firing the coax instead of the main gun on near targets, a practice that continued to be used in tanks until recently.

   The assistant driver, placed beside and to the right of the driver, operated the gimbal-mounted light machine gun placed in the tank's front or "bow." Tanks used these until the mid-1950s.

CHAPTER 7. BREAKING THE JAPANESE BARRIERS

1. Dick Turpin, "New Marine Club: Flashback to WW II," *Los Angeles Times,* March 6, 1983.
2. This was most likely Col. Walter J. Stuart, commander of the 2d Marines, attached at the end to the 4th Marine Division.
3. "Thrilling Story of Tinian Landing and Battle with Japs told by Marine Major Robert Neiman," *(Mount Vernon) Daily Argus,* October 7, 1944.

CHAPTER 8. INFERNAL IWO

1. Starting with Iwo, all C Company tanks had names starting with C, B Company, names starting with B, and so forth.
2. We liked our LSM crew so much that we left them one of the two jeeps we "borrowed" from the army after Saipan—one on that island and one while we were in port in Honolulu.
3. Shutt later got in trouble with the navy censors for sending the film to Eastman Kodak for processing. Technicians there referred it to the authorities. I think that I saved him from being court-martialed with my paper defense of him. See *V for Victory: Iwo Jima, Okinawa, and the Push on Japan* (n.p.: Acorn Media, 1991).
4. C. B. Ash to author, November 20, 2001, copy in author's possession.

CHAPTER 9. OKINAWA

1. This incident remains known as the "Father's Day Massacre" among veterans of the 1st Tank Battalion who fought on Okinawa. Although only two tanks were hit, all the crewmen were casualties.
2. Bob Boardman, *Unforgettable Men in Unforgettable Times* (Seattle: Navigators, 1998), 186–96.
3. The OY was a Piper Cub derivative employed by the navy. It was similar to the army's L-4 "Grasshopper" observation aircraft, which was used primarily for artillery spotting and to take senior officers up for a view of the battlefield.

EPILOGUE

1. I suspect that this project either did not become a film, or that it was passed to Michael Blankfort, who wrote the screenplay for *Halls of Montezuma* for Darryl F. Zanuck, which was released in 1950.

INDEX

ISBN 1-58544-240-2

9 781585 442409   90000